# CONFESSIONS OF A
# RECOVERING FUNDAMENTALIST

# Confessions of a Recovering
# FUNDAMENTALIST

*Keith Ward*

CASCADE *Books* • Eugene, Oregon

Cascade Books
An Imprint of Wipf and Stock Publishers
199 W. 8th Ave., Suite 3
Eugene, OR 97401

www.wipfandstock.com

PAPERBACK ISBN: 978-1-5326-9671-8
HARDCOVER ISBN: 978-1-5326-9672-5
EBOOK ISBN: 978-1-5326-9673-2

*Cataloguing-in-Publication data:*

Names: Ward, Keith, 1938–, author
Title: Confessions of a recovering fundamentalist / Keith Ward
Description: Eugene, OR: Cascade Books, 2019
Identifiers: ISBN 978-1-5326-9671-8 (paperback) | ISBN 978-1-5326-9672-5 (hardcover) | ISBN 978-1-5326-9673-2 (ebook)
Subjects: LCSH: Christian philosophy | Theology, Doctrinal | Religion and science | God—Christianity | Jesus Christ—Person and offices
Classification: BT75.3 W21 2019 (print) | BT75.3 (ebook)

Manufactured in the U.S.A.                                    OCTOBER 17, 2019

All Biblical references are from the New Revised Standard Version

I am very grateful to Marian Ward and Dr. Robin Parry for deleting my worst jokes and modifying some of my greater exaggerations

# Contents

Introduction  vii

**CHAPTER ONE: HOW TO DEAL WITH THE BIBLE  1**
Escaping from Hell  1
How God Morally Improves  5
Strange Experiences and Magic Books  7
Good News and Bad News in the Bible  12
Dancing with John Wesley  16

**CHAPTER TWO: WHAT IS GOD?  22**
Fuzzy Theology  22
What Was God Doing before Creation?  26
Minds without Bodies  28
Can God Ride a Bicycle?  30
Unfortunate Events  33
How to Grow a Universe  35
Souls, Persons, and Potatoes  38

**CHAPTER THREE: HOLDING INFINITY
IN THE PALM OF YOUR HAND  43**
Playing Superchess  43
Cucumbers, Bread, and Wine  47
Why Jesus Is Better than a Cucumber  51

**CHAPTER FOUR: DEALING WITH EVIL  56**
Dangerous Figs  56
Does God Grow?  60
Living in Sin  64
Looking for a Good Religion  67
Why Did Jesus Die?  70

**CHAPTER FIVE: WHAT CAN WE KNOW ABOUT JESUS? 76**
Where Did Jesus Go? 76
Was Jesus Real? 79
Extraordinary Events 85
Mozart and the Prophets 88
Looking for the Cosmic Christ 89
Am I the Only Person Who Is Right? 92

**CHAPTER SIX: COPING WITH THE CHURCH 94**
How the Churches Began (Possibly) 94
The True Church, or Perhaps Not 98
The Importance of Water 103
Begettings and Proceedings 105

**CHAPTER SEVEN: DEATH AND AFTERWARDS 110**
Life after Death 110
What Will We Be Like after We Die? 113
Is There a Hell after All? 116

**CHAPTER EIGHT: BEING IN A MINORITY 119**
Living with Difference 119
Conclusion 123

*APPENDIX:*
The Nicene Creed—What Most Churches Say They Believe 127

# Introduction

IF ANYONE HAS READ any of my other books, this one may come as a bit of a surprise. It is something completely different. It has been said that a philosophy could be expounded purely in jokes. I have often wondered if the same could be said of theology. So I thought I would try it. The result is a bit odd. It is based on true events, but they have been partly disguised and exaggerated. It is meant to be a serious but light-hearted look at the state of Christianity in one place at one point in time. It contains quite a lot of what are meant to be jokes. It also has some serious stuff mixed up in it, and I hope you can tell the difference!

Is theology a suitable subject for jokes? I think that God is so great, so incomprehensible, so far beyond human understanding, that a sense of humor is needed with regard, not to God, but to anything we humans presume to say about God. Believers shouldn't always take themselves too seriously. Maybe humor can take some of the sting out of the more quarrelsome and angry disputes that have marred the face of Christian faith. I think religion ought to be fun, something life-enhancing and joyful, anyway.

All theology, and all philosophy, is written from a specific point of view, and there is no point in disguising that. My point of view is that of an Anglican (a member of the Church of England, which is a member of the world-wide Anglican communion, including many national Episcopal churches), at the beginning of the twenty-first century specifically, and I am quite happy to be in that place, even though lots of things about it also make me quite annoyed.

Though I speak from that viewpoint, I try to take as wide a view of religion, and of Christianity, as possible, and I try to make sense of my view in the light of modern science, the critical study of history, the great changes in moral outlook in recent times, and some of the changing fashions in modern philosophy. Those are the serious bits.

What I say may surprise some; it may shock some; it may make some despair that this form of religious faith exists at all; and it may make others glad that religious faith can take such a form. If you are not religious, it may give you a good laugh. If you are not Christian, it may give a surprising view of what Christian belief can be like. If you are not an Anglican, read it as a confession of what a minor official in this religious society is allowed to think (or at least gets away with) at this point in time. If you are an Anglican, forgive what I have mocked and please know that, as Shakespeare put it, "if we offend, it is with our good will."

# CHAPTER ONE

# How to Deal with the Bible

## ESCAPING FROM HELL

LIKE MANY PEOPLE, I was converted to Christian faith (or re-converted or, they might have said, "properly converted') by a group of very literalist Christians—people who are often called 'fundamentalists." They never really got me to do as they did, waving my arms in the air and shouting out that I loved Jesus a lot—I was always a rather introverted and undemonstrative character. Still, they did get me to commit my life to Jesus and to believe that Jesus was somehow living as a spiritual reality, and was able to change my life, my feelings, and my basic motivations, goals, and hopes, from within.

It happened in a rather unusual way. I was serving in the Royal Air Force in the Persian Gulf, where it was very very hot. On the base where I was sent, there was only one air-conditioned building. It was the Chapel. So I spent a lot of time there, just to get out of the heat. The Chapel also had an organ (well, a harmonium really), and since I could play the piano, I soon became the organist (the harmonium has no pedals, so it was easy) for the Chapel services. You might say that I came to play, and I stayed to pray.

This little group of charismatic Christians caught me as I was seated one day at the organ, and cajoled me into praying with them. The bottom line is that after a few sessions I did have a spiritual experience. At first I thought it might be indigestion, but I could not get rid of the feeling that it was an experience of the risen Christ calling me to follow him. I still think it really was that. I still know some of those charismatic Christians, and I am

1

proud to call them my "fathers in God," and I still admire their faith, their commitment, and their devotion to God in Christ.

But do I admire all that they believed? I have to say "no." Over the next few years I moved further and further away from many of the things they believed, without ever losing that first thrill of a new relationship to God through the person of Jesus Christ. I am what is often called a "recovering fundamentalist," and I must admit that I don't want to recover completely.

The first break with their beliefs was when they told me that my father was going to be punished for ever in hell because he didn't accept Jesus as his Lord and Saviour. That seemed to me a bit much. My father wasn't perfect, but he didn't deserve to be punished—well, not too much anyway. There were one or two things he did that he should perhaps be brought to account for, especially when he hit me with a slipper. But to be punished *for ever*? And to be punished because he didn't believe what I believed? *I* would not do that to my father. So how could a God who was supposed to be merciful and loving do it?

These are old questions, of course. Still, they made me wonder where my friends had got their idea of eternal hell from. They thought they got it from the Bible, and the Gospels do report that Jesus said that at the end of the age there would be a judgment when evil people would be thrown "into the furnace of fire, where there would be weeping and gnashing of teeth" (Matthew 13:50). There's lot of weeping and tooth-gnashing in Matthew's Gospel. I think Matthew must have been quite a grumpy old man.

I have now come to think there are two important things to bear in mind about stories like this, which Matthew in particular is very fond of. One is that they are stories, not predictions. They are obviously not *literally* true—there is no furnace (maybe in Saudi Arabia?) in which millions of people are still conscious and spend their time gnashing their teeth. Still, even if it is not literally true, this imagery seems to point to something pretty unpleasant.

The other important thing is that nothing is said about how long they have to gnash their teeth, or about whether they will ever escape from the furnace. So maybe my Dad would only have to gnash his teeth for a few years, and then could go and cool off in the nearest river and get some new teeth. Or maybe the story is just saying in a very poetic, if rather gruesome, way, that people who do evil things will pay for it in some way sooner or later. It's true that Matthew, being the grumpy person he is, at one point talks about "eternal punishment" (Matthew 25:46). But we need to think about this. The Greek word translated as "eternal" is "*aionios*." That does not necessarily mean "for ever." It literally translates as "for an aeon" or "age-long." That sounds like a long time, admittedly. But maybe the contrast is between the time of this world, which brings change and decay, and a different sort of "unearthly" existence, where time does not pass in the same way. Then "eternal life" would be life in a different sort of time, where there is no decay, no loss of the past or fear for the future, a life beyond suffering and tears. And "eternal punishment" would also be existence in a different sort of space and time, which would be much less attractive. In both cases, the emphasis is on the *sort* of existence (the relation to, or the separation from, the Eternal God) rather than to a specific length of time.

Other images that Jesus uses for this state are "the outer darkness," being shut out from a great feast, or a "prison" where you are shut in until you have paid the last penny. Fire, darkness, and prison are not something to look forward to. When ministers take funerals, even of notorious criminals, they do not usually say, "Our dear brother departed is unfortunately now going either into a fiery furnace or into outer darkness or into prison, I cannot tell you which. Either way, it looks like he is in for a hard time. It is, I am afraid, all very depressing. Let us pray."

But maybe there is a glimmer of hope, after all. The fire, the darkness, and the prison may be "eternal"—that is, in a quite different time and space from this one. But, even if the fire and the prison exist for ever, there are hints that there may be a way out—people may pay the last penny (Matthew 5:25–26), or be purified "as if by fire" (1 Corinthians 3:12–15), or eventually get a chance to go to the Feast after all (Matthew 25:12—Jesus locked the ten foolish maidens out, and said, "I do not know you." But maybe later on he remembered who they were and let them in. Or maybe there would be other feasts to go to later, when the maidens had found some oil). Then there is the mysterious statement in the Book of Revelation (everything is mysterious in that book) that hell (the text says "Hades") would deliver up the dead, and hell would be "cast into the lake of fire. This is the second death" (Revelation 20:13 and 14). Does that mean that hell itself dies, and is destroyed? Who knows? It is worth nothing, however, that in the same book, unsettling and cryptic though that book is, it says that the leaves of the tree of life are "for the healing of the nations" (Revelation 22:2), and that "the kings of the earth will bring their glory" into the open gates of the New Jerusalem—all of which might imply that even these "kings," who had opposed Christ and his people (Revelation 6:15; 17:2, 18; 18:3, 9; 19:19,

*[margin note: 'noting' surely?]*

21), might have a chance of forgiveness and new life. There is a hint of hope here, even for fundamentalists.

There are more than hints. Didn't Jesus, after he died, "descend into hell"? If we go back to 1 Peter 3:19, where this seems to be mentioned in the New Testament, in Greek the word "hell" is not used. (That word is actually not used anywhere in the Bible.) In this case, it is "prison," which, even though it is not very nice, is not as bad as a Pieter Bruegel painting. And what it says, at least in one place, is that "the gospel was proclaimed even to the dead, so that, though they had been judged in the flesh as everyone is judged, they might live in the spirit as God does" (1 Peter, 4:6). It is possible that Jesus' sermon just told them they were stuck in prison for ever. But that would be a pretty depressing sermon (and hardly sounds like "the gospel"—unless you have severe sadomasochistic tendencies). It rather looks as though Jesus preached even to those who had been condemned to punishment so that they might not be stuck there for ever. When they have done their time, and repented, they could get out.

Why should I think this? Simply because I think the Jesus I experienced was a merciful, loving, reconciling, person who was prepared to give his life for others, and went to the furthest possible lengths to reconcile humans, even evil humans, to God. The God of unlimited love he talked about could not possibly punish people without hope of reprieve just for what they did in one short human life. If we are supposed to love our enemies, God cannot do less. The God who says "love your enemies" must surely care for the well-being even of those who are God's enemies. Well, that's what I think, and I hope God agrees.

Jesus certainly talked about judgment on evil. People have to be held responsible for what they do. But the Jesus I experienced came with "good news," not bad news for most people, and offered forgiveness and reconciliation to God. He even in some way took the judgment on himself—he "died for me." So the final word about God is not judgment; it is forgiveness and reconciliation.

As I came to think more about these things, it became obvious to me that I could not really continue to be a full—what they called a "Bible-believing"—member of a church that took the Bible in a very literal way. I had to find another way of reading the Bible, and I had to find some church that accepted such a way. This was harder than you might think, because the literalists seemed to hold the high ground in almost every church I came across.

4

## HOW GOD MORALLY IMPROVES

The irony is that my fundamentalist friends brought me to know and love a Jesus who offered unlimited forgiveness of sins, and yet they believed in a Jesus who sent people to endless punishment without any hope of reprieve. I see how they got into that situation. They read the Bible literally, even though Jesus mostly spoke in parables and hugely exaggerated metaphors. And they interpreted the Bible in a very savage and judgmental way (as many Christians have done, unfortunately). God was a severe Judge who demanded punishment for sin, and would not hesitate to mete out that punishment when the time came. I would not call a human being who did that sort of thing "loving." So I certainly would not call a God who does that a "loving God."

As I thought about these things, it seemed to me that it was possible to read the Bible in a very different way. You don't have to say that everything in the Bible is true, and literally true most of the time. If you do that, you ignore the fact that the Bible is a collection of different documents—histories, laws, proverbs, psalms, prophecies, and stories. They were written by many different people over a period of many centuries, and they express many different points of view, from the facile optimism that everything is for the best ("happy is everyone who fears the LORD," Psalm 128:1) to the depressing view that almost everyone is sinful and doomed ("There is no one who does good, no, not one," Psalm 14:3). But some people try to read it as just one book that conveys one consistent set of beliefs, all of which are equally true.

If God was going to write a Bible, the least he could do would be to write it all in one language, and definitely not in Hebrew, which has no vowels, thus leaving people to guess what it actually says, much of the time. He would write it all in the same style, and provide some footnotes and a few references to explain the obscure bits. I would expect no less of any human author, so it is not too much to ask of God. If the Bible was submitted for a PhD, it would surely fail. Fortunately, God is probably not in need of a doctorate!

My fundamentalist friends would say that if an early writing in the Bible says that God told the Israelites to massacre all the Amalekites, including their children and cattle, then God really did say that (Deuteronomy 25:17). In other words, God is sometimes in favor of genocide, at least of people God doesn't like. It is a bit difficult to see how such a God is very like the God Jesus talked about, who is merciful and requires love even of enemies (Matthew 5:43). Did God take a course in moral philosophy between Deuteronomy and Matthew? Something certainly seems to have changed.

I think the obvious thing to say is that it was not God who changed. It was people's ideas about God that changed. Early in history, some spiritual leaders in the Hebrew tribes thought that God was a savage and dangerous figure, who destroyed nearly everyone in the Great Flood, who killed people in earthquakes because they had worshipped idols, and zapped anyone who touched the Sacred Ark or walked on the Sacred Mountain. We know that many tribal societies are in awe of a dangerous God who savagely punishes people if they break the taboos or walk into sacred spaces. The early Hebrews were no exception, and the Bible contains records of many such practices and punishments. It even contains hints that child sacrifice was sometimes practised by the Israelites, though the prophets disapproved of it.

What the Bible seems to record is a long, slow development of ideas about God. God gets more morally just. In the early days, he punishes everybody indiscriminately, but later on, according to the prophet Ezekiel, he only punishes people who are personally guilty (Ezekiel 18:4). God becomes more a God of mercy and justice than a God of strict vengeance for ritual offences. God becomes a being who prefers moral action to the offering of animal sacrifices (Amos 5:21–24). You can see this development taking place in the Old Testament. Jesus took the development even further when he saw God as a God of unlimited love, who would go to any lengths—even to sharing in human suffering and death—to reconcile people to the divine life.

Jesus' view of God was new and revolutionary. But it was the development of a long Jewish tradition, and the Old Testament can be seen as the story of this development in human understanding of God. If we take the teaching of Jesus seriously, we are almost forced to see the Old Testament as recording ideas of God held by people who only gradually come to see God as truly good, benevolent, and loving, and as a God who loves all creatures rather than just one set of Middle Eastern tribes.

If that is what the Old Testament is, we should expect the many different documents—four Gospels and many letters—of the New Testament to be of the same sort. They are written by different people with different points of view, and they record their slightly different understandings of Jesus, and the ways in which he challenged and transformed their ideas of

God and God's purpose for the world. We can get a good idea of the person of Jesus, but we see it from different points of view, and as strongly influenced by the preconceptions and prior beliefs of the people who edited or compiled and wrote the documents that now make up the New Testament.

Despite this, you can see how a fundamentalist who tries to take all the Bible as literally true might think that God is a God of vengeance and strict retributive justice. This God chooses to be merciful to a small number of people, selected more or less at random. God decides who they are—you will probably think they are Roman Catholics if you are Roman Catholic, or snake-handling Baptists, if you are one of those, and you haven't been bitten yet. Then God exempts his chosen band from destruction—"saves" them—and everybody else just has to put up with it and be damned.

My friends told me that when I committed my life to Christ, I was "saved," and if God decided to punish my Dad for ever, I just had to put up with it. Well, at that point I decided not to put up with it. I did not reject God or Jesus Christ. I rejected the view that God and Jesus were vindictive, immoral, and irrational superbeings. And so I had to reject any view of the Bible that suggested that God was like that. I had to have a different view of the Bible.

Fortunately, it was easy to do—though it is always difficult to escape completely from the fundamentalist ideology, once you have been part of it. What usually happens is that you tend to keep falling back into bits of it, even when you are not aware of it. Many of us always have to be on the lookout for fundamentalist fossils in our thoughts and beliefs.

## STRANGE EXPERIENCES AND MAGIC BOOKS

I must admit that I have never understood why the vivid and life-changing personal experience of God in the person of the risen Christ so often goes along with regarding the Bible as a sort of magic book, miraculously preserved from all error, and telling you all you need to know about God, life, and everything. After all, the earliest Christians did not even have a New Testament to appeal to, and Jesus never wrote a book, so it is rather odd that Christians have regarded an infallibly revealed book as essential to their faith. You would think that if Jesus had wanted us to believe in an infallible book, he would have written it down himself. But all he wrote was written in sand (when the woman taken in adultery was brought before him; John

8:6), and we do not even know what it said! It probably said something like, "How am I going to get out of this?"

I puzzled and puzzled about these things. Then one day came the thought that freed me from all the problems I was having with the faith of my friends. It was a thought that was obvious, really, but I had not thought it. The thought was that the real center of Christian faith must be the person of Jesus, as he is experienced as a present spiritual reality. *The Christian revelation of God is in a person*, a living, breathing, dynamic, complex person. It is not primarily in a book whose words are unchangeable and which presents all sorts of intellectual puzzles as we try to make all the different bits of it consistent with one another.

Of course, if we identify that spiritual and personal presence as "Jesus," it must be rooted in some historical figure. We must have some authentic idea of what Jesus was like. Now you can see where things can begin to go wrong. It may be argued that if we need to know what Jesus was like, there must be a record, with no mistakes in it, of exactly what he was like and repeating exactly what he said. This is where literalism gets going. But this is where fundamentalism is fundamentally wrong.

The fact is that we can never be absolutely certain about what anybody is like. Even when we think we know somebody quite well, other people will disagree with us about what they are really like. There will be some things we might agree on—when and where they were born, what job they did, and how they related to their friends. Even then, there might be disagreements. Some people might think a person was dignified and learned, whereas other people might think the same person was pompous and pretentious. But at least no-one who knew that person would think she was flippant and ignorant. There are limits.

When we are thinking about dead people, things get worse. Memories fade and tales about them get exaggerated. My wife and I are capable of arguing for hours about whether we first met on a Monday or a Tuesday. And I actually have some memories of doing things that only she did, or so she tells me. Memory is not very reliable. And we do tend to exaggerate things for effect. I used to remember being in a traffic jam for over an hour on the Washington Beltway. After a few years, that jam had grown to over three hours. When I told the story last week, I was stuck on the Beltway nearly all day. The story just grew and grew, all by itself.

When we read medieval accounts of how saints flew through the air or, like the wonderful young maiden St. Uncumber of Norwich in England, grew a beard overnight to preserve her virginity (I won't go into details), we take them with a pinch of salt. Yet we might think that the saints in question certainly made a dramatic impact on people, that they were believed to be genuinely outstanding spiritual teachers, and that they have come to stand for something of value in human life, something that meant a lot to people. But they didn't grow beards overnight!

The stories of Jesus in the Gospels might sometimes be exaggerated or slightly misremembered, but they were written by people who all believed that Jesus was the expected Jewish Messiah or liberator, who had ushered in God's kingdom in a new way, the way of the Spirit.

The really decisive thing is that Jesus was believed to be alive in the presence of God, and to be encountered as a vital spiritual reality in the experience of the disciples.

If you ask a Christian the question, "Whom do you encounter in your spiritual experience?" the answer is, "The risen Christ." If you ask, "How do you know it is Christ?" the answer is, "This reality is the transfigured and glorified form of the historical person of Jesus, whose life is portrayed from four different points of view in the Gospels." Actually, I don't suppose any normal person would say that. Nevertheless, that is all you need. You do not have to go on to say, "And what's more, those Gospels contain no mistakes at all."

Just in case you are getting worried, I should say that I do not think every Christian has to feel that they have had a very dramatic personal encounter with Christ. But I do think that such experiences are very important to take seriously. Probably most Christians—especially Anglicans—have a more gradual and restrained sense of the presence of God that does not cause them to jump about and shout a lot. But they would hope for a closer knowledge of God, at least after they are dead. In the meantime they are happy to grow gradually in faith, without being plagued with sudden bouts of enthusiasm. And they would probably agree that the great saints do have an intense sense of the presence of Christ. So, experience of a spiritual presence is at the heart of Christian faith, even when it takes a very civilized and undemonstrative form. And that experience does not have to rely on any infallible texts or infallible people.

I have never understood why anyone should ask for infallibility. I think it is probable that the Gospels are correct in most of what they say about Jesus (though if you were not a Christian you would probably see more legendary elements in the Gospels). But it is much less probable that the Gospels contain no mistakes or differences of opinion at all—human memories and human books are just not like that. If you read the Bible carefully, you will see that the Bible is not like that either, because there are quite a lot of differences of opinion in it. Just try getting the date of the Last Supper right. Was it at the Passover Feast of before it? Different Gospels give different answers, so unless there were two Last Suppers, at least one of the accounts is wrong. A small difference, to be sure, but if there is any difference at all, infallibility goes down the tubes.

Anyway, if you say you know the Bible is true because it is infallible, you are faced with the much more difficult question of how you know it is infallible. After all, it does not say it is, in so many words. And if somebody else says it is infallible, how do they know? They would have to be infallible as well. (I will come to the pope in just a minute.)

Religious believers often try to escape the fact that most of our beliefs are just based on probabilities by saying that the Bible is certainly true, because God wrote or at least dictated it. But that is just to say that you *think* God dictated it. And that is yet another probable belief—with which many intelligent people disagree, and which cannot be established beyond reasonable doubt, so it can hardly be certain.

One of the most celebrated people in the world to be infallible is the pope. But how does anyone know that? Because the pope said so. But when the pope said he was infallible, was he infallible? If not, then perhaps he made a mistake. I personally, as an Anglican, think that he did make a mistake, and so do nearly all Protestants and Eastern Orthodox Christians (and not a few Roman Catholics, though they usually keep rather quiet). It is just not a good argument for something being true that the person who said it told us that he (or she) could not possibly be wrong. The fact is that when he said that he was probably wrong.

Anyway, the pope is only infallible on very rare and special occasions. Nobody knows exactly what these are, but it seems that it is only when he speaks "ex cathedra" (from the Papal chair), defining a doctrine that is part of the deposit of faith of the apostles (there are supposed to be no "new revealed doctrines") on behalf of the whole church. If you look on the internet, you will find that some people, who call themselves "traditional Catholics," think that there are no less than 255 infallible declarations. But they are just making this up, as they cannot be certain that the pope was properly seated on his chair at the time, so they just make a list of doctrines they happen to like. Because they have called themselves "traditional

Catholics," the list is very long, and goes into details most people, and most Catholic theologians, have never thought about.

Most Catholic theologians agree that there are basically just three declarations by the pope that are without doubt infallible. One of these is the definition that the pope is infallible, so that does not count. The other two are the bodily assumption of Mary into heaven, and Mary's immaculate conception. Since none of these are in the Bible, and hardly anybody knows what the second one about Mary means (most people seem to think it means that Jesus was conceived without a human father, which it doesn't), it is not very likely that they are part of the original faith of the apostles. (The pope is presumably supposed to know that they were part of the original apostolic faith, even though they have been unaccountably either forgotten or hotly argued about for centuries by everyone else.)

I have officiated as a priest at an Anglican church dedicated to the Blessed Assumption, so it is possible for Anglicans to accept at least two of these declarations. On the other hand, most parishioners called the church in question the church of the Unwarranted Assumption, and that probably reflects what most Anglicans think. The whole thing is complicated by the fact that it has sometimes been hard to know which person is infallible. There have been times when there were three popes, and they could all have said that the other two were not infallible. On this occasion, I think they would all have been correct (but not infallible).

At present, as I write, there is an emeritus pope, and perhaps he wanders around the Vatican muttering sadly, "I used to be infallible, you know, but now I'm not so sure." Meanwhile, the actual pope can say, "Well, I used to make mistakes, but just look at me now." Maybe the answer is to get the pope never to sit on his throne and speak "ex cathedra" again—one pope actually promised to do this. Then it will not matter whether the pope is infallible or not. That would be very helpful. Of course, the pope could say, "I now infallibly declare that I am not infallible." That might be a bit confusing! Yet it is not much worse than saying, "I now declare that I am infallible," which to be honest simply sounds rather pretentious.

If no person is infallible, perhaps the Bible is—though the Bible is written by persons, of course. If you knew that God personally wrote the Bible, then of course it would contain no mistakes. But why on earth should you think God wrote the Bible? We have seen that there are problems with the Old Testament, written without any vowels and in lots of different styles. The New Testament books are not much better. They are written in very indifferent Greek, and again in very different styles. If God wrote them, wouldn't God have been better at Greek grammar? And wouldn't God have written them all in the same style just to assure us that God had written it? Might God not have put in a few differential equations or perhaps something like the Theory of Relativity, just to prove that he knew everything.

If you mean that God inspired people so that they remembered some of the striking things Jesus said and did, influenced others so that they collected many sayings into Gospels, and influenced some committee to choose some of these Gospels to go into something they called "The New Testament," then that may well be true.

It is the Gospels that give us the only real information we have about Jesus. That is why the Gospels are really important for Christians. But there are four different Gospels. The fact of these differences is very important. God could perhaps have provided just one completely coherent biography of Jesus. Or Jesus could have written one himself. But that is not what we have. We have four differing accounts of the effect Jesus had on some of his disciples.

## GOOD NEWS AND BAD NEWS IN THE BIBLE

Where does that leave us? My literalist friends would say that the Gospels give a totally inerrant account of what Jesus did and said. All the Gospels are consistent with one another, they say, and the words ascribed to Jesus in the Gospels are just what Jesus said. To believe anything else, they have told me, is to put the Christian faith in danger, and to betray Jesus.

Those are strong words, enough to frighten anybody who does not want to betray Jesus. My friends are the nicest people imaginable, yet these are words that put a great deal of psychological pressure on people to accept their view of things. "Either you agree with us," they say, "or you will probably suffer for eternity with your Dad." That is a fate that is literally worse than death (sorry, Dad).

I have a Bible at home called The Good News Bible. I have always liked it—it has little pictures in, and it is written in clear straightforward English. But one day in a bookshop I came across another book called *The Bad News Bible*. Some Bibles put the reported sayings of Jesus in red print, to make them stand out. But *The Bad News Bible* put in bold red print all the really bad news that the Bible contains for most of the world's population. The bad news is that God will come with terrible vengeance to destroy the earth and to condemn millions of people to a dreadful death. This may be good news to the small number of the elect (144,000, some say). However, it is very bad news to everybody else.

Actually, when you come to think of it, it's not even good news to those who are "saved," not if they have any love or compassion for all their friends who are going to be fried for ever in the fiery furnace. Surely they'll feel pity and sorrow for their friends. I would certainly feel sorry for my Dad. I could never be really happy if I knew he was still suffering, with no hope of release. I suppose I would have to pretend to be happy, or they would throw me out. But I would really be quite sad.

Were my friends really saying that if my Dad didn't join the church (or if he joined the wrong church—i.e., not theirs) he'd suffer for ever? The more I thought about it, the more it seemed to me that a God of real love would never say, "I love you as much as possible; but if you don't do just what I tell you, and believe just what I say, I regret to have to tell you that I will punish you for ever." There must be a better idea of God than that.

Well, there is a better idea, and it is in the Bible. The first letter of Timothy, in the New Testament (1 Timothy 2:3) says, "God, our Saviour, *desires everyone to be saved.*" If that's what God desires, God will naturally make it possible for everyone to be saved. Since most human beings have never even heard of Jesus, if God makes it possible for them all to be saved, there must be some other way than by accepting Jesus as your Saviour.

My position, as I finally arrived at it, is this: there are lots of different ideas in the Bible, even within the New Testament. They cannot all be true, so you have to say: these are the ideas different people had when they encountered Jesus, either during his life, or as a spiritual presence afterwards (the "risen Christ"). They are not all equally accurate. Why is that? Because what people see depends quite a bit on what they themselves are like. If they are a bit grumpy, like Matthew, they see quite a bit of judgment and being thrown into furnaces and quite a lot of gnashing of teeth. If they are a bit soft-hearted, like Luke, they see things like prodigal sons returning home or good Samaritans being held up as ideal models to follow. Mark is a plain-speaking type who says, "Just give me the facts," and sees Jesus as the expected Messiah or "anointed Davidic King" who will usher in God's kingdom, probably quite soon. John sees things from a very different point of view, from the point of view of eternity—he sees the eternal Word or Wisdom of God becoming embodied in Jesus.

The Gospels, though they are obviously all about the same person, are very different from each other. Matthew has no prodigal sons; Luke has no gnashing teeth; Mark has no mysterious sayings about Jesus, God, and his disciples all being one; John has no great interest in Jesus as the Jewish Messiah. There is a good reason for that. It is because their own personalities led them to concentrate on different bits of Jesus' teaching.

I prefer Luke, but I admit that I ought to think about tooth-gnashing more, since it is probably based on something Jesus taught, whatever it means. If you ask me to make a general assessment of Jesus, as he is pictured in the Gospels, I will look at these four different pictures and explain the differences between them as due to the different personalities of the collectors and editors of the Gospels. They were dealing with memories of a real person, who was at least as complicated and hard to understand as other people are, and giving us their point of view, thinking specially of the difference he had made to their lives.

When I make a picture of Jesus for myself, I am doing the same thing. I see him as a white man with a small beard (though probably not with glasses and false teeth, even though they would be very useful for gnashing), who speaks about God in Elizabethan English (the language of the Authorised Version of the Bible, which naturally is completely correct), and is very interested in philosophy. He is, to be honest, rather like an improved version of me. I am seeing him from my point of view, with all the things my education has taught me and all the cultural baggage and personal prejudices that I carry with me. What we actually get is not one totally agreed and comprehensive account of Jesus. What we get is a range of reactions and perspectives to a mysterious but absolutely charismatic figure, which challenges us to add our own perspective to the mix.

Some things are pretty basic. Here was a man who challenged the hypocrisy of the religious leaders of his day, who ate and drank with notorious sinners, who healed those who were physically and mentally ill, who taught that people should turn to God, because God's rule ("the kingdom") had drawn near, who warned that evildoing would be judged severely, but that sincere repentance would reconcile even the worst sinners to God. He died on the cross because he remained true to his mission of showing that God's love excluded no-one, and because he fearlessly criticized religious and political authorities for their arrogance. Many of his disciples claimed that they saw him in some form after his death. Then they were apparently filled with the Spirit of Christ, which gave them renewed faith and inspired them with hope for the triumph of goodness in the end.

My faith is not that there is a book that reports lots of facts but never makes any mistakes. My Christian faith is basically that there was a person, Jesus, who showed by his life and teaching that God is a being of unlimited mercy and love, who will judge and ultimately eliminate evil, but who desires that everyone should come to know and love goodness, truth, and beauty, and find fullness of life and true happiness by conscious relationship to the personal spiritual presence that is the true and living God.

To believe this we do not have to believe absolutely everything in the Gospels. Nor do we have to believe everything Paul and company wrote in their letters, which make up most of the rest of the New Testament. No doubt they were all "inspired," in the sense that their minds were raised by God to new insights and experiences. Hardly anything could be more inspirational than Paul's great declamation that "now faith, hope, and love abide, these three; and the greatest of these is love" (1 Corinthians, 13:13). On the other hand, not many things could be worse than the declaration of the second letter to the Thessalonians (probably not by Paul, thank goodness), that Jesus will appear from heaven "in flaming fire, inflicting vengeance on those who do not know God, . . . they will suffer the punishment of eternal destruction" (2 Thessalonians 1:8 and 9—"eternal" is that word "*aionios*" again, so their punishment might not be for ever). That is where the literalists get their God of vengeance and destruction from. I guess the Holy Spirit tried very hard with the writer of that second letter to the Thessalonians to get him to moderate his very human desire for vengeance on those who were persecuting Christians. But in this case even the Spirit did not completely succeed.

There have certainly been lots of Christians who have thought, and who still think, that Jesus' God is a God of vengeance who will send unbelievers to hell without hesitation. I have come to totally reject that idea of God. I think it is a hangover from very much earlier ethical ideas, and it has been eliminated forever by the Johannine teaching that "God so loved the world, that he gave his only Son" to redeem it (John 3:16).

There are lots of literalists in the Anglican Church, and I am not against them being there. I am all in favor of freedom of belief, at least until beliefs start hurting other people. But I do wish they would stop saying that they are the only real Christians, and that the rest of us are betraying Christ. As a matter of fact, I found that most people I met in the Anglican Church were not literalists. On the whole, they were people who liked music and choirs, jumble sales and garden fetes, singing psalms, and sitting down and standing up in church when they were told, and generally doing good in quiet ways. As for the Bible, they generally think it is a very good thing, but not many of them read things like the Book of Leviticus or take too seriously the biblical command to look for Amalekites and exterminate them (Deuteronomy 25:19), perhaps because there are no Amalekites left, or at least nobody who admits to being one.

## DANCING WITH JOHN WESLEY

If we do not have an infallible Bible is there any authority, you may say, that we can base our beliefs on? Well, you can have perfectly good authorities without them being infallible. Einstein was an authority on physics, but I would not have asked him when Caesar crossed the Rubicon. He was not a historian. He even made some mistakes in physics, but was still a great authority—he knew much more than almost everybody else.

I would expect the same would be true in religion. Some great saints or great writers know much more about God and how to know God than anybody else. Jesus certainly did, but he is not around anymore. What we have are about two thousand years' worth of people who claim to have experienced God through Jesus, and who have reflected on their experiences and those of other spiritual teachers. The testimonies of those who lived near to the actual historical Jesus will be especially important. They will be able to guide us as we seek to know God through Jesus. But none of them need to be infallible.

The trouble is that there seem to have been lots of different beliefs around, even in the very earliest records. Many early Christians thought that all Christians (all male Christians, that is) should be circumcised (Acts 15:1); the apostle Paul did not. The issue was not settled until what is usually called the first church council, when Paul won the day. However, that was only after a long argument, so it seems pretty obvious that Jesus had not made any definite ruling on the point—or if he had, that the disciples did not hesitate to make their own minds up. Many Christians (Arians, at one time the majority group in the church) thought Jesus Christ was great, but not quite as great as God. Others insisted that he was God. Some thought Jesus was omniscient and omnipotent. Others thought no human being could be quite as great as that.

There is a way to solve that problem. All you have to do is to find a definitive authority that will tell you what the correct beliefs are. That sounds good, until you realize that you do not always agree with what the chosen authority says. Roman Catholics say that in the end the Bishop of Rome is the person who gets it right (though they thought of this rather late in the day, and only after a lot of arguments). Eastern Orthodox Christians say that it is the ecumenical councils of the church, the first six or seven general councils, before Roman Catholics split off from what was then the main group of Orthodox Christians. Some Protestants say it is the Bible (as interpreted by them, of course, not by people like Catholics). Other Protestants say that they cannot think of any definitive authorities except the local minister, and he or she always seems to differ from the minister down the road.

All this tells you is that a lot of people desperately want a definitive authority to tell them the truth about Jesus and about what they should believe. But it also tells you that there are lots of competing claims to being a definitive authority, and each one usually ignores the others, though sometimes one person will burn another at the stake just to demonstrate his (it's almost always a "his") own superior spiritual state.

Does the Anglican Church have any authority? Not much, it would seem. Going back in relatively ancient history, there are the 39 Articles, which in 1562 were laid down for members of the Church of England "for the avoiding of diversities of opinions." That never worked, because people would insist on having lots of diverse opinions, but for many years people had to sign up to those Articles if they wanted a respectable position in British society. All religions change over the years, and very few people would now hold exactly the beliefs that were current three or four hundred years ago. Luckily Article 21 says that even the most solemn Councils of the Christian Church "may err, and sometimes have erred, even in things pertaining unto God." That implies that the undoubtedly much less important councils of the Church of England may err and have erred as well. Some of those errors may well be in the 39 Articles, so that dispenses with them as any sort of final infallible authority. Anyway, the 39 Articles of the Church of England are now of little more than historical interest for world-wide Episcopalians. Phew!

I would think that the leaders of the Anglican Church have a certain authority for Anglicans, because they are usually old and have been thinking for a long time. But they can also be pretty silly and short-sighted, they don't like change very much, and I have never met an infallible one. What authority they have is usually exercised in very gentle way.

I had the privilege of being present at the inquisition of an Anglican priest in England who did not believe in God. That may seem very far out for a priest who prays to God every day, but very few things are beyond the ingenuity of Anglicans. The inquisition was conducted by the Archbishop of Canterbury, and a few other bishops and some theologians. It went something like this:

(Archbishop to the accused) "Would you like sweet or dry sherry?"

"Dry sherry, please." The assembled dignitaries breathed a sigh of relief. He had made the right choice, and was clearly not a hopeless case.

That having been settled, the conversation continued: "They tell me you do not believe in God."

"That is true. God is not an object that exists and can be pointed out in some way."

This produced a murmuring among the theologians. Eventually one said, "What do you mean, God is not an object? The Bible says that God 'rode upon the clouds,' so he must have been some sort of object."

"Were those real clouds, do you think? And was God was lighter than air?"

"Ah, a point well taken. I do not suppose God was actually riding on the clouds. Probably it is an allegory for the divine presence with the army of ancient Israel."

"Quite so. The clouds are allegorical, and so is God. Allegories are not objects, after all."

And then they fell to a long discussion of the meaning of allegory, and of the meaning of the word "object," and of whether allegories could be objects, and if so, what sorts of object they would be.

An hour or so later, they had decided that there was much controversy about whether God was an object, and if that was what the accused meant by not believing in God, it was indeed a permissible theological opinion. After all, he still used the word God, as in "My God, what is going on?" or even "Oh My God," which he had actually been heard to say at various points during the discussion. These, it was generally agreed, were not statements about the existence of supernatural objects, but ejaculations of deep emotion—which was very suitable for a pious person, though not used too loudly or enthusiastically in church, not in Anglican churches anyway.

So the evening ended amicably, with everyone feeling they now knew much less about objects and allegories, but they had experienced many mysterious and satisfying emotions in the course of the discussion.

It may sound woolly-minded, but this may be preferable to the sort of Inquisition that used to be practised by the Dominicans in the ages of good old traditional faith, which involved the use of various instruments of torture instead of glasses of sherry. I should say that the Dominicans do not do that sort of thing any more, though regrettably they prefer whisky to sherry.

Perhaps because of their addiction to sherry, Anglicans are sometimes accused of not believing anything in particular. This is not quite fair. They do believe some things, but find it hard to remember exactly what they are, and even harder to work out what they mean. In general, if not in particular, they tend to believe that it is quite a good idea to have a pope as the leader of the universal Christian churches, but wish he was not quite so infallible. They tend to accept the doctrinal definitions of the first six ecumenical councils, but reserve the right to interpret them in quite new and unexpected ways. They tend to accept that the Bible is the word of God, but think that the word is rather too long (as the editor of the *Readers' Digest Bible* said, as he cut the Bible down to a more digestible size) and it contains many obscure bits, and quite often wanders into realms of fantasy, though there is always something worth thinking about even then. They do like Jesus a lot, but they do not see the need to be too enthusiastic about it. They go in for baptism and Holy Communion, but would rather not go into technical details about exactly what is going on while such rites are in progress.

It is true that the Anglican Church has come into existence through a series of accidents, and that its historical origin with the Church of England might have been avoided if the pope had been a bit more understanding about divorce and remarriage (he managed that in many other rather similar cases, after all). Once it existed, however, it continued because of various other complaints about the authoritarian practices of the Roman Church, though it was not above indulging in some authoritarian practices of its own.

After a few years—a few hundred years, actually—it had settled into being a rather tolerant body that managed to embrace a number of different Christian points of view. It has no pretensions to be "the one true church," but it does think it is part of the worldwide company of disciples of Jesus, in many different forms, which is the one true church, and it probably suspects that it is actually rather a good part.

I think that this attempt to include many sorts of Christians and to allow many sorts of interpretations of the Christian tradition is rather good. It may make the church look rather fuzzy, but a fuzzy faith seems to be just right for the present age, which is full of fuzzy people. When religious and philosophical doctrines get too precise and hard-edged, conflicts tend to grow fiercer, compromises are harder to achieve, and intolerance and opposition looms.

When I say fuzzy, I do not mean that you should be satisfied with superficial beliefs. I mean that when you really explore the hardest philosophical beliefs—like the existence of free will, the nature of mind, the nature of causality, or the nature of the laws of nature—you begin to realize that there are no easy answers and no way to answer your questions that will satisfy everyone. It's not that your brain is fuzzy (though it probably is). It is the basic ideas themselves that are fuzzy, that evade precise definition, and that cannot be tied down in neat phrases.

Just try defining "God," and you will see what I mean. It is not that it has no meaning. It just has too many possible meanings, and none of them seem totally satisfactory. Maybe God is a perfect being, but what do you mean by "perfect"? Maybe God is the creator, but what do you mean by "creation"? Philosophers are even capable of arguing about the meaning of "meaning," so they need to ask what you mean by "what do you mean" before they can get started. It is not surprising that meetings of philosophy faculties in Western Universities hardly ever get started. The members cannot agree about what exactly is meant by an "agenda," and by the time they have discussed that in enough detail, it is time for dinner.

All in all, there are some sorts of authority in the Christian faith that I am happy with. There is the authority of the spiritual experiences of many holy and wise people ("experience"). There is the authority of the Bible as showing the development of the idea of God among the Jewish people, and then, for Christians, giving various reflections of the impact Jesus made on many of those who knew him ("revelation"). There is the authority of the writings of generations of wise and thoughtful Christians, as they thought about their faith ("tradition"). And there is the authority of scientists, historians, and philosophers who investigate our changing knowledge of the world in which Christian faith exists ("reason").

This little list is sometimes called the "Wesleyan Quadrilateral," which is unfortunately not a dance performed by Methodists, though it was, apparently, based on the thought of John Wesley, and is still used by some Methodists. It is quite enough authority for anybody, but none of it needs to be infallible. It is the basis upon which each person can work out a faith for themselves—or, of course, which may lead them to think that this faith is not for them. For me, it has just the right degree of fuzziness to counteract my remaining fundamentalist tendencies.

# CHAPTER TWO

## *What Is God?*

### FUZZY THEOLOGY

So HERE IS A bit of fuzzy theology. The main difference between this and what some Christians say is that I know it's fuzzy and inadequate, whereas some Christians seem to think that they know (and I used to suspect that *I* knew) something about God and Christ that is clear, precise, and totally adequate and correct.

Looking back at my own Christian commitment, it began with a vivid experience of Christ as a spiritual reality, which changed my life for the better. I felt I could never deny the reality and importance of that experience. But I also felt the need to place it in the context of a wider worldview within which it made sense. For a start, I would have to believe in God, or there would be no spiritual reality as I had experienced it. Then I would have to believe that there was a living Christ, who had some relation to the historical person of Jesus. I would have to believe in a divine Spirit which was somehow present within me. And I would have to believe in the possibility of a new and more fulfilled life in union with God.

This is not like a list of theoretical beliefs that I have to sign up to if I am to call myself a Christian. I have no interest in dividing the world into true believers versus heretics. It is more like an attempt to set out what must be presupposed if I am to accept my initial experience as authentic. Such an attempt, as far as I am concerned, should meet the four conditions of the Wesleyan quadrilateral. It should be based on real spiritual experience (experience); it should accept that there is a revelation of the nature of God in the person of Jesus (revelation); it should pay attention to the reflections

22

and experiences of other Christians, building up a tradition or set of traditions of Christian thought (tradition); and it should take account of the
best established knowledge of the nature of the world that is available at the
time (reason).

One of the earliest attempts to do this was the so-called Nicene Creed,
developed from an original that came out of the first major ecumenical
council of the church, the Council of Nicaea, in 325 AD. It sets out, very
briefly, the nature of God, summarizes what the Bible says about Jesus,
makes a remark or two about the divine Spirit, and adds that Christians
believe in forgiveness and the hope of eternal life with God. It adds some
difficult stuff about how Jesus was "begotten, not made," and was "of one
substance with the Father," and of how the Spirit "proceeded" from the
Father (the Latin church later added "and from the Son," which became
quite contentious). The Creed also mentions the "holy, catholic [meaning
universal], and apostolic" church. It does seem to be a presupposition of
anyone's becoming a Christian that there should be some continuing body
of disciples that can preserve the Christian experience of regeneration
through Jesus Christ. However, the original Anglican version of the Creed,
found in the Book of Common Prayer, dropped the word "holy," after looking more closely at its clergy and congregations, and deciding that they did
not look very holy.

These modifications are all in need of some attention, as they are
closely tied to controversies of the day that have now receded into history
and have been largely forgotten. Nevertheless, this creed has become the
most generally accepted statement of Christian faith that is actually used
in services of worship. If only for that reason, it is worth looking at it again,
in the light of our very different background philosophies and scientific
knowledge of the world, and seeing whether it needs to be made a bit fuzzier in parts.

I have put the Church of England 1662 Prayer Book version of the
Nicene Creed as an appendix to this book, just to check. Since I have now
finished reading my own book, I know it will turn out that I can accept a
fairly fuzzy version of this creed, and so I can still say it in church without
leaving my brains at the door. But it will also turn out that my version will
be rather fuzzier than many people would like, and it will certainly include
some things that nobody at Nicaea could possibly have thought about.

Anglicans have, on the whole, accepted the Nicene Creed. At least
they say it at every communion service—sometimes they sing it, which is

better, because you don't have to worry so much about believing what you sing. I recall Professor R. B. Braithwaite, an eminent professor of philosophy at Cambridge, who wanted to be baptized in the Anglican Church as an adult. When told that he had to say the Creed, he protested that, as a good Logical Positivist, he did not believe it. He was, however, prepared to sing it. So there must be a difference. If there is a basis for Anglican beliefs (and maybe for the beliefs of most Christian churches), the Nicene Creed is it—as long as you interpret it in a suitably fuzzy way. How fuzzy would I have to be? I shall just have to see.

First of all, the Creed starts by saying there is God, described as "the Father almighty, maker of heaven and earth." Every word of this phrase, except for "the," "of," and "and," needs to be fuzzified. "Father" is a major problem in Western secular societies these days. Whereas in ancient times women tended to be shut up in a cave having babies, men could be warriors and hunters. Men were generally the dominant protectors and providers, and so it seemed natural to think of the creator, who never had any babies, as "Father of the universe."

Not any more. The subjugation of women is one of the scandals of human history, and we need to be clear that not only has God no brain; God also has no testicles. The Jews were aware of this, and insisted that God was not physical, and that brains and testicles are physical things, so God has not got them. Partly for this reason, all pictures or images of God were forbidden in ancient Israel. Nevertheless, in the Bible God is often referred to as "he," and a main reason for this was that worshippers of goddesses in Palestine were often prone to sexual orgies and various scary practices, often involving testicles and other bodily parts, to ensure fertility. But I do not think that sort of thing is a real consideration today (though I confess I am not quite sure what happens in Britain at Stonehenge on summer nights).

There is, of course, no reason why goddesses should be more sexually active than gods. Greek and Roman gods are nothing if not sexually active. I have never understood why some opponents of women priests say that if we had women priests, we would have sex at the altar. Does that mean male priests have no sex? Roman Catholic priests are not supposed to have sex, though in one Spanish village I know of, the local priest lived in the same house as his housekeeper and her children. Everyone in the village called the priest "Father," except the housekeeper's children, who called him "uncle." There was no sex involved, of course.

Enough about sex. We just need to be clear that God has no gender. Anyway, for whatever reasons, males have dominated females for most of human history, and this is hopefully coming to an end in some parts of the world. If calling God "Father" has contributed to this, that is shameful.

But part of the Christian life is devotion, a profound personal relationship to God, which is mediated to Christians through the person of Jesus. Jesus was undoubtedly a man, so this image of God is male. What we need to do is not to get rid of the male image of God, but to get rid of the idea that being male is equivalent to being dominant and superior. Since Jesus said that he who would be great must become the servant of all (Luke 22:26), we have a good precedent for this. The man who gave his life on the cross is not a dominant alpha male, the leader of a wolf pack who imposes his will on others by force. Jesus gives us a re-imaging of maleness, and that might actually be good.

Another thought is that the word for Spirit is feminine in Hebrew, and neuter in Greek, so it is quite possible, and maybe helpful, to think of the Holy Spirit as feminine. That way, you need no longer think of the Holy Trinity as two men and a pigeon (Father, Son, and Holy Spirit) but at least as two males and a female. That might help. But it might not, since males would still outnumber females two to one. Then you can try pointing out that Jesus was the incarnation of the eternal Logos, which is certainly not male. In fact, since Logos is the Wisdom of God, it too would be feminine in Hebrew. That looks more like a draw—in God there would be one and a half males and one and a half females.

This is beginning to sound like theological hair-splitting at its worst. It is better just to say that theologians have never really thought that God had testicles, and that many Christian writers have sometimes referred to God in feminine terms. Jesus apparently referred to the Creator as "Abba," which was the common Aramaic term for father (it did not mean "Daddy," as some have misleadingly said). So it is more important to de-stereotype fatherliness, accept that these images have understandable, if often deplorable, historical origins, and get on with cultivating a real personal relationship with God, without thinking that God has to fit into some human gender-category.

## WHAT WAS GOD DOING BEFORE CREATION?

Is God a person? Some people say so, but I do not find that convincing. The trouble is the word "person" is intrinsically fuzzy. Maybe, being in favor of fuzziness, I should like that. But I fear it may be the wrong sort of fuzziness. It may induce people to think that God is really rather like a superhuman being.

I blame Michelangelo for this. He actually painted God on the ceiling of the Sistine Chapel, and his God is like an old, white, very large human person. Michelangelo was wrong. We have to get away from that picture. God is the "maker of heaven and earth." For the ancient quarrelsome theologians of Nicaea, heaven was the spiritual realm where God lived, and it was filled with angels, archangels, and other spiritual eminences (I do not think they had a spiritual pope). Earth was where we live, the center of a very small universe, with the suns, moon, stars, and planets orbiting around the earth.

We now know that this old picture was wrong. It was far too small. It is actually only since the twentieth century that we have known that there are a billion stars in the Milky Way, with billions of planets, and a billion galaxies in the visible universe, and that the universe has been expanding ever since it started, about fourteen billion years ago with a Big Bang (this was shown by a Roman Catholic astronomer and priest, Georges LeMaitre, in 1925, so it is definitely not anti-Christian, though it does mean we have to take the Genesis six-day creation account as a myth).

The universe is almost unimaginably huge and old, and it may well contain many alien forms of extra-terrestrial life. Humans are a tiny part of the universe, nowhere near the center—we are near the rim of a rather small galaxy, and if we all blew up tomorrow most of the rest of the universe would hardly notice.

God is the creator of this huge universe, so God is not likely to look anything like an old male human being. And there is another thing. When God created the universe, God did not sit around for a long time thinking, "I wonder whether I should bring something apart from me into being." Then God thought, "It might be quite nice to have somebody to talk to," and then God decided to create the universe. It took God six days to complete the job and then, feeling exhausted, God had to have a rest on the seventh day.

That is more or less the story you get in the Book of Genesis. But actually "creation" is not the beginning of the universe. God did not start the whole thing going, and then leave it to get on by itself, apart from the occasional interruption to punish people God did not like.

"Creation" is the dependence of the whole physical universe, all the stars and galaxies, even the whole of space and time itself, on something beyond it. That something is *beyond spacetime*. It not only has no brain and testicles, it is *not in space*—we could not reach it by travelling in some direction, however far we went—and it is *not in time*. Time began with the Big Bang, and before that there was no time. That means there was nothing "before" it, because there was no time before the first moment of time.

When the fourth-century theologian St. Augustine asked himself what God was doing before time began, he answered, "Before there was any time, God obviously wasn't doing anything, as God just didn't have the time." For him God was therefore timeless. Since all changes take time—there is a before and after—God must also be changeless. And if God is changeless, nothing that happens in time can cause any change in God, so God is also impassible. This word is so unusual that my computer keeps crossing it out and replacing it by saying "God is impossible." My computer also consistently replaces my phrase "God is the first cause of the universe" by the phrase "God is the first curse of the universe." I suspect that my computer is an atheist!

Anyway, to say that God is impassible does not mean that God is the fastest thing in the universe, which nothing can ever pass. It means that God cannot be affected by anything that happens in time. For instance, if somebody on earth prays and asks God to do something, God will have to say, "Don't you realize I am changeless? There is nothing I can do." It also means that God can never do anything new. A changeless being cannot ever have any new ideas, cannot respond in new ways to things that happen in time, and cannot help people in response to their difficulties.

This is very odd. But it is important to see that this is probably the traditional Christian view of God. It is not much like seeing God as a person who can have a change of mind, can respond to prayers, and can even enter into time as a human person. No wonder many people find the Christian idea of God hard to swallow. It seems to be a combination of the idea that God is timeless, changeless, and unmoved by anything that happens in the world, with the quite different idea that God answers prayers, becomes human in the person of Jesus, suffers and dies on the cross, and can do anything, including new things that even God has never thought of before.

## MINDS WITHOUT BODIES

Luckily there is a way to sort this out, though it is a way that only really became openly talked about by theologians after the sixteenth century, and is still thought by many (probably by most, to be honest) to be controversial.

You start by saying that God is the creator of spacetime, so God is beyond spacetime. You can think of something that could exist that is not in space. That is a mind or consciousness that has no brain or body. You can easily imagine such a thing. Stand in front of a mirror and look at your reflection. Then imagine your arms disappearing, then your legs, then your body, and finally even your head. You become an invisible man or woman. Except that your whole body has completely ceased to exist. But you are still there seeing the mirror (which is now empty), hearing noises and smelling whatever smells there are around.

You can have all these sense-perceptions even though you have no eyes or ears or anything to produce smells. You can also have feelings and thoughts. You can do sums, and ask yourself if you still exist without your body. Some people actually have these experiences, when they find themselves in a hospital operating theatre looking down at their body from above. They still have a body, but they are not using it.

I agree this would be surprising if it happened to you. But you can *imagine* it. It is not completely impossible, you just don't think it will happen. You can even imagine changing bodies, and finding yourself thinking the same sort of thoughts you always did, but having quite a new body. There are lots of films about this sort of thing. The novelist Kafka wrote a book in which a man's body changed into that of a large beetle in the night. His wife was quite upset.

Anyway, the point is that you can image a mind that exists beyond space; if you ask where it is, the correct answer is that it is nowhere. But why should everything be somewhere? That is just prejudice. So, we can suppose that there is a mind beyond space. When you say it is a mind, you mean that it has awareness, it knows things, it feels things, liking some and disliking others, and it is capable of thinking. It might even be capable of doing things, bringing about events in space just by thinking.

Why not say that God is a bit like that? But God is a supermind, who knows everything, every state that could possibly exist; who likes some of these states (happy and beautiful states) and dislikes others (painful and ugly states); and who has the power of making some of these states exist just by thinking about them and willing them to exist.

28

The supermind is not in space, but it can bring a space like ours into existence. Is it in time? This is a bit harder to imagine. It would not be in our spacetime, because in our universe space and time are connected very closely to each other. Our universe's time began to exist at the Big Bang. But—and here is the key point—our time is not the only possible sort of time. If there is a disembodied supermind that thinks one thing after another, then that is a sort of time. It is not physical time, because the mind is not physical. It is mental time. By that we just mean that in this mind one thing can happen after another. Not all thoughts have to happen at the same time.

You can imagine the supermind thinking, feeling, and changing. You are not stuck with a mind that can never change and can never be affected by anything else. You have a mind that can wonder what possible states to create, can decide to create some of them, and can then be changed by observing these states. It will have to be changed, because first of all there were no actual states for it to observe, and then there were some. Something has changed, and the supermind observes it.

Just by imagining, you have solved the problem about how God can both be beyond our spacetime and yet can have a sort of mental time that enables God to change, make new decisions, and respond to things it creates. This is so obviously a very good idea that I cannot understand why everyone does not agree with me. All I can say is, they don't, despite the fact that I am obviously right (remember, however, that I do accept that we are all a bit fuzzy, so I may not be completely right. But I still think I am more right than they are).

I can now answer the question: what is God? God is a supermind beyond our spacetime who can do what might sound like four impossible things before breakfast. But they are not impossible for a disembodied cosmic supermind. First, it will know all possible states of affairs. Second, it can sort them into good (desirable) and bad (undesirable). Third, it can make some of them actual (create a universe or two). And fourth, it can then observe and respond to them. It can do many other things too, and we will come to some of them later.

Now we can begin to see how we can have a personal relationship with this God. As the supermind observes what we do, it knows what it would like us to do (what we have been created for), and it can respond to us to try to encourage us to do those things, and maybe also to correct us when we fail to do them (when we "disobey God's will"). We humans have a degree of free choice, and we can decide what to do and think. But we are always influenced by the presence and the thoughts of others. It is only natural that we will be influenced by the presence and the thoughts of God. That sort of influence—knowing what others think and what they try to teach us, and knowing that they share and are influenced by what we do and think—is a personal relationship.

We may think that being beyond spacetime is a long way away. But actually, since God is nowhere (physically speaking), God is not a long way away at all. The cosmic supermind, if there is one, can influence us all mentally and directly by a form of supertelepathy. And because it really is extremely super, it can take an intense interest in everything in the universe. It can do huge numbers of things at once, without ever getting tired or losing the plot.


## CAN GOD RIDE A BICYCLE?

This God is absolutely amazing. Carrying on with the Nicene Creed, it says that this God is not just amazing, God is almighty. Theologians have struggled with this one. Many of them have said that God is omnipotent, meaning that there is nothing God cannot do, that God can do *absolutely anything*.

There are some obvious problems with this definition. Can God ride a bicycle? Can God get married? Or—a favorite one, this—can God create a stone that is so heavy that even God cannot lift it? The first two questions seem pretty easy to answer. God could create a bicycle, create a body, and make that body get married on a bicycle, if need be. Even then, however, God could not have exactly the same feelings as a person getting married on a bicycle would have. A person on a bicycle would always be afraid of falling off, whereas God could be absolutely sure God never fell off. So, God could never have exactly the same feelings as a human being, because God could never be a human being and God at the same time.

At this point, you might suddenly think of Jesus, and say, some people think Jesus was a human being and God at the same time, so what about that? As politicians say, I am glad you asked me that question, let me talk about something else instead. I will just say for now that even if Jesus was filled with fear in the Garden of Gethsemane, then God was not filled with exactly that fear. This needs a little more thought, but I haven't got time to go into it now.

Let me go on to the very heavy stone problem, which I am sure is what everyone really wants to know. I think that is fairly clear: God can lift any stone, so God could not create a stone God could not lift. There are some things God cannot do. QED. Making a generalization from this obvious case, we can now say that God cannot do anything that contradicts the divine nature (which includes being able to lift absolutely anything).

That seems to me a perfectly good answer. But it has a drawback. Since God is such an amazing supermind, it seems most unlikely that we could ever know just what the divine nature is. So, as far as we can tell, there may be thousands of things God cannot do, because the divine nature is what it is. In that case, God will not be omnipotent after all.

The really hard question about God for many people is why there is so much pain and suffering in the world. If God knows all possibilities, knows which are good and which are bad, and chooses which ones to create, it sounds as if God must have chosen lots of bad possibilities. Because bad things certainly exist—people dying of cancer, in earthquakes, in wars, and in epidemics of disease. Is this because God likes to see people and animals suffer? That doesn't sound like a very good God.

Suffering is a terrible thing, and I wouldn't want to come up with some abstract theory that makes it seem less bad than it is. After thinking about it for a long time—all my life, nearly—I have come to the conclusion that some suffering, and some really bad suffering, is just a necessary feature of the way things are. By saying it is necessary, I mean there is no alternative; it cannot be avoided.

God creates, brings into existence, everything in heaven and earth, everything that exists anywhere, in any universe. It may be that God has to create some universe, that it is part of the divine nature to create a universe, that there is no alternative. Philosophers put this by saying that God creates some universe by necessity. It is not a matter of free choice.

Maybe God has some choice about which sort of universe to create, but it is not a totally free choice. Maybe any universe that God is able to create and that is good enough for God to create has some suffering, some bad states, in it. God does not choose the bad states, but God has to choose some universe with bad states in it. God has no choice about that.

We are no position to say why there have to be bad states in every universe that could be created. We can make some guesses, like saying that if there are going to be successful violinists, there just have to be lots of unsuccessful violinists. That may seem rather trivial, but I assure you it is not trivial to lots of violinists who spend all their lives trying to succeed, but never make it. And it is also annoying for lots of people who have had to listen to their efforts.

Again, there are many people who like dangerous sports, and they have to accept that risk of injury and death are part of what they have chosen to do.

These are just rather superficial examples, but you can see how, if there is going to be a universe where it is good to strive hard to achieve good things, there will just have to be possibilities of failure as well. I am just suggesting that, if we could see how good and bad are interwoven, we might get a faint idea of how no universe, at least no universe of the sort we live in, could exist without some suffering and badness in it. Perhaps no creatable universe could eliminate the possibility of evil.

I propose, then, that the cosmic supermind has a restrictedly free choice in creation. It has to create some universe, any universe it can create will contain evil, so the choice will be between the sorts and degrees of good and evil that possible universes contain.

If this is a coherent view—and I believe it is—then God is not strictly speaking *omni*potent. States will exist in any created universe that God does not choose, and that are just bad. They are not means to a greater good, and they are not all due to sinful choices made by creatures. They are just unavoidable. Even God cannot avoid them. God just has to do the best God can in the circumstances.

This may seem a rather feeble God. My school report used to say, "He has done the best he can; indeed, he is not capable of doing any better." My mother always thought it was a very good report, but I knew the truth. It meant I was a boy of limited abilities. Is God like that?

Well, yes. But there are two main qualifications. First of all, there is nobody who has more power and wisdom than God. God is the most powerful being there could possibly be. I think that is what "almighty" means. It means that *God is the greatest possible power, and all power comes from God.* There is no other being who could have such great power—the power to know and create this vast universe in all its amazing complexity and structure. It wouldn't, after all, be bad if my abilities were limited, if my school report had added that nobody could possibly ever, in the whole universe, have greater abilities than me. My mother, of course, thought that is what it meant.

Secondly, God is not limited by something other than God. The limits are set by God's own nature, which God cannot contradict. There is not an alien hostile power against which God has to struggle. It is the divine nature itself that decrees that the universe must develop in the ways it does, perhaps in order to find a destined fulfilment through hardship and persistent endeavour.

## UNFORTUNATE EVENTS

Does this mean that God is not good? It does not mean, as some people apparently think, that God is like a kindly old gentleman who does not want his children to come to any harm, and will protect them from anything that threatens them. Some Christians speak as though their God is like that, but they still die of cancer or heart failure or get killed in earthquakes.

Such people sometimes make things worse by then saying that the evils they suffer are punishments for their sins. The ultimate refutation of this appalling view was the great Lisbon earthquake of 1755. In that terrible event, which killed thousands of people, many Christians sheltering in churches were killed, while the Red Light district, full of prostitutes, had most survivors. The trouble about the "suffering is a punishment for sin" view is that almost always the wrong people suffer. The pious and charitable poor die because they cannot get out, and sinners have enough sinfully acquired money to escape to safer places.

The fact is that evil arises from God, who is the ultimate source of all reality ("everything in heaven and earth"). In that sense, God is beyond good and evil. It is not possible to judge God by our moral standards, because many evil, as well as many good, things arise from God by necessity. Human minds have to work with their given personalities and capacities, which they do not choose. So, the ultimate divine mind has a given nature, which it does not choose, which is just there, and not caused by anything beyond it (there is nothing beyond it).

The philosopher Bertrand Russell, even when he was a little boy, thought he had a knock-down argument against this God. If everything has a cause, he said, and God is the ultimate cause of everything, then what caused God? He must have been a very annoying little boy, especially in Sunday School. What he failed to see is that it is not true that everything has a cause. What you should say is that everything that comes into being has a cause (is brought into being by something else). Scientists do generally accept this. But suppose there is something that cannot come into being. It is just always there. Then obviously nothing can bring it into being, so it can have no cause. So there, Bertrand Russell! God either exists or does not exist. But God cannot begin to exist—and God cannot cease to exist either.

Here, then, is a bit more we can say about God. God is a mind that is eternal—it cannot come into being or be caused by anything else. God just always is, eternal mind. Worlds arise from God, as various possible states that God's mind contains press into actuality. That is just what they do. Even God just has to put up with it, and so do we.

But, like us, God is free within limits, even though God is restricted or limited only by the eternal divine nature. A free mind is a mind that can think of possible futures, and choose between them. Such a mind will always choose what it thinks is good, which is worth having, which is not painful or boring. We cannot imagine any rational person choosing something just because it is painful or not worth having. Human minds often do choose things that are painful or boring, but that is because they are stupid. They do not mean to be in pain or bored. It is just that the things they choose—like eating lots of sugar or playing cards all day—lead them, sooner or later, to be in pain or bored stiff.

God, being a supermind, is not stupid, and will choose things that really make for happiness and fulfilment. It is obviously good to be happy oneself, and to know about and share in the happiness of other beings. So that is what we would expect that a rational supermind would bring about. Therefore, to the extent that God is free and rational, God is a power making for goodness and happiness. The problem is that this is not a world in which all beings are good, happy, and fulfilled. That needs some explanation. If all things arise from God, and if all the things that God freely intends are good, then it seems that there must be some things that arise from God that God does not intend. Those things must just arise from God by necessity, not by choice. God cannot help it.

Oddly enough, modern physics helps to explain how this might be so. Most scientists agree that the fundamental laws of nature (like the force of gravity) have to be exactly what they are if intelligent conscious beings (like us, or some of us) are ever going to exist. But if there are such laws, they will sometimes cause harm to conscious beings—they will produce earthquakes and volcanic eruptions. Such unfortunate events are necessary if the planet is to remain a stable place for life, but that stability is ensured at a cost to some of those lives. What this shows is that certain kinds of conscious intelligent life can only exist if some dangerous and harmful events exist. We humans are one of those kinds. We are beings who take risks, go on adventures, who develop, grow, and discover through effort and persistence, who reach maturity by endurance and persistence. Why God should create beings like us, when he probably could have created hosts of happier and cleverer beings, is a bit of a mystery. Perhaps God did create such beings, but they are not in this universe. We are beings who can only exist in this universe, of which we are integral parts. Either we exist in a world like this, or we do not exist at all. If you complain that God should have created a more perfect world than this one, it might be fair to point out that God could have done that, but you certainly would not have been in it. You would not have been at all.

A little knowledge of physics helps us to see why carbon-based intelligent life-forms like us can only exist in a world of very finely tuned and generally predictable laws, which is bound to be a risky and often dangerous—though also an intelligible and beautiful—world. Even a cosmic supermind would have to accept that.

This may seem like a pretty weak God, compared with the God that many people believe in, who can do absolutely everything, and is in total charge of the universe. But I cannot see, and I do not think anybody can see, how that Total Control God could put up with a world with so much suffering in it. I prefer a weak but well-intentioned God to a God who could stop all the suffering in the world, but refuses to do anything about it.

In any case, it is probably not fair to call God weak, when this whole amazing universe all depends on God for its existence. This is a God of immense power as well as a God who intends and aims at good. And I think the right way to think of it is that any universe God creates will contain many good things that otherwise would never exist, and it will end up with an absolutely overwhelmingly good outcome, in which Christians believe that all creatures will be able to share.

## HOW TO GROW A UNIVERSE

This is where Christ comes into the picture. I am not talking about the human person of Jesus here, even though Christians think the human Jesus is the Christ. By "Christ" I am referring to what the Gospel of John calls the "*Logos*." That means the reason, wisdom, or thought, or "word' of God. We are still thinking about God as eternal mind. When we think about minds, we think about the thoughts that minds contain. We have imagined that God thinks about every possible state that could ever exist, and some of these states are good, some bad.

We do not know what God thinks about all day, and God certainly does not think in the way humans do. We think about one thing after another, we often make mistakes and indulge in very bad arguments and illogical trains of thought. God is very good at logic and is always right. This would be very annoying if we tried to have an argument with God. It would not be a good idea, even though the Bible says Abraham and Moses both tried it.

Some of God's thoughts are about possible universes, whole sets of states that are interconnected in very complicated ways. Among these universes, there are some that we might call "evolutionary universes." An evolutionary universe is one where you start with very simple elements. They slowly develop, becoming more complex and structured, until they unfold all the possibilities that were hidden within them at the start—well, maybe not all, since some possible states will conflict with others. But a lot of them anyway.

Think about the birth of human beings. They start off with one cell that gets fertilized. These cells grow and develop, passing through many stages, until they form a recognizable human shape. They develop a nervous system and a brain, and eventually they begin to think and feel. From a simple cell a thinking, feeling, conscious mind emerges. This is an evolution, a development from simple to complex, from unconsciousness to consciousness, from physical to spiritual.

Now think of the universe as being like that. It starts simple, with the Big Bang, before there are even any subatomic particles. Then it becomes more complex and structured. You get photons and electrons, then atoms, then molecules, then DNA, then brains, and conscious intelligent and morally free persons. This is an evolutionary universe. Somehow the development of societies of intelligent sentient beings is implicit or potential in the very first simple stage of the universe.

When we bring God into this picture of an evolutionary universe, we can see that one of the thoughts in the eternal mind is the thought of that fully developed universe. That universe has developed through many stages from simple to complex, from physical to spiritual. The thought of the final goal was there right at the beginning of the process. It is a bit like an architect's plan of a building, which guides the whole process towards a goal that is already present in the thoughts of the architect, but still needs to be realized by a whole lot of builders.

Here comes my suggestion about how to think of Christ: Christ is the eternal thought of the final goal of an evolutionary universe. The thought ("the word") is there in the eternal mind right at the beginning, and it is the plan that guides the whole process. This seems to fit the beginning of John's Gospel perfectly: the thought (the *Logos*) was with God before the beginning of this universe, like a thought is with its thinker. And the thought was God, just as a thought is a part, or an expression, of a mind.

If we can go along with this, then we can see that God is not weak at all. God plans a particular evolutionary universe, and the universe follows that plan. So, God does not do the best God can in a universe that God does not control at all (as if God might try hard, but never totally succeed). God does control the universe, but not totally. That is because one important thing about an evolutionary universe is that it is in important ways self-built.

Building workers erect a building in accordance with an architect's plan. But they are doing the work, and they might have to make adjustments here and there. They might even depart from the plan, though that usually ends in disaster. They have to use the building materials that are available, and they might have to face storms and floods, and work hard to get the building finished on time. Some of them might give up and go for a drink. But the architect, though she cannot interfere too much with the work of building, will probably manage to see that something very like her original plan gets built. Then everyone can relax, and maybe even live happily ever after in what they built, being especially pleased that they have largely built it themselves.

In an evolutionary universe, the builders are actually part of the building. They are sentient beings that seek to implement the plan in ways that they understand (and they may not be very good at reading plans). Especially near the beginning of the process, there will be nobody who can read the plans very well. The building itself is like a gradually developing organism. It is something of a cross between a growing baby and a building under construction. All sorts of things can go wrong, but something new and original, designed by an architect but modified by building workers, gets built in the end. And maybe the architect (Christ) can finally step in to see that everything ends well.

The story is obviously getting quite complicated. But what do you expect, if we are trying to talk about the whole history of the universe? At this point, however, we might look back at the idea I mentioned earlier of universes just popping out of the eternal mind almost at random, leaving God to do the best God can, which might be very little. We need to revise that from a Christian point of view, and say that universes do not pop out at random, or of their own accord. God does have plans for universes— maybe many different plans for very different universes. These plans are all good. They are all concerned with the construction of final goals of great value. All the universes God plans have a purpose and great value. They are designed to go somewhere, and one way or another they will get there.

But the building sketched in those plans has to be constructed by workers and with available materials. This is where the limitations built into the divine nature kick in. Especially in a self-developing evolutionary universe, there will inevitably be suffering and dead-ends. The workers might be lazy or unreliable, and the materials (the set of possible states in the divine mind) may contain many potentialities for bad as well as good states. So, the whole picture is of a planned universe that will certainly end in an overwhelmingly good state, and that is guided towards that good at many points, but from which all evil, suffering, and waste cannot be eliminated, even by God. If that picture makes sense, then God is good, even if God is nothing like a kindly old gentleman, but more like a cosmic mind that has to create some universe, plans a hugely good outcome for the universe God chooses, but has to work with a load of grumpy workers (that is, finite sentient minds) and a lot of mixed-quality materials (that is, possibilities in the divine mind with many diverse potentialities). One of the unique features of such an evolutionary universe is that the workers will make their own contribution to what happens. Furthermore, these workers will be increasingly conscious and mark increasingly creative stages in the self-realization of the possibilities and of the general goals that God has put into the universe from the start. God is not the Total Controller, but the enabler of the creative and responsible choices of created and developing minds.


## SOULS, PERSONS, AND POTATOES

I think that the idea of an evolutionary universe is quite helpful if you want to make sense of the world we live in. Yet some Christians seemingly have trouble with evolution. They think that only human beings have souls, and are much more special than animals, which do not have souls, and which God apparently does not care much about. Some Christians even think that humans are the most important things in the whole universe ("the crown of creation," one text says), and therefore that they cannot have evolved from mere animals.

This is a very weird view. Human beings are animals on a rather small planet in a relatively small galaxy. They do, on the whole, have some properties that many animals on this planet do not have, like the ability to solve differential equations or to give lectures on moral philosophy. Actually, not many humans have those properties, but I have to admit that I have never seen a chimpanzee at my lectures on mathematics. On second thoughts, I am not quite sure about that, but I would hesitate to say so on my term reports.

The Bible does not say that only humans have souls. Indeed, it explicitly says that animals as well as humans possess 'Neshamah,' Hebrew for the breath of life (Genesis 1:30), and a related word is 'Nefesh' (living being), which is often translated as "soul," and which also includes animals. The philosopher Aristotle said that even potatoes have souls. Of course, they have potato souls, which do not do very much except grow and reproduce. But that's not a bad start for a soul. Animals have a slightly more developed sort of soul, which is conscious and is able to move around much better than potatoes. Then humans have "intelligent souls" (minds), which sometimes do mathematics and go to lectures.

It looks as if souls gradually evolved from whatever very simple souls potatoes might have, through the more complex souls of insects and birds (dinosaurs, though very large, turned into birds, and had very small brains), to dogs and cats (which most British people, at least, think have souls), through to the higher primates, among which we can count humans. The development of souls is connected to the development of brains, and they are more or less the same thing, even though I have shown (at any rate to my own satisfaction) that the conscious experiences, thoughts, and feelings that higher animals have could conceivably exist without brains. More of that later.

Some dogs, their owners say, are very intelligent, and biologists sometimes say that humans are not at the top of the tree of life. Humans are just branches, along with other animals. So, it may seem there is nothing special that sets humans apart. Yet it is hard to imagine even a very intelligent dog worrying about the meaning of life, asking itself what it ought to be doing in life, and then setting out to do it as well as possible. In medieval times dogs sometimes used to be put on trial for wrong doing, and held guilty or innocent. That does not seem fair. We train dogs, but do not give them lectures on moral philosophy, or ask them if they really know the difference between right and wrong.

This is what seems to make humans special, even though these days we might want to say that some other animals, especially the great apes, should be treated as moral agents too. Even then, there is a big difference of degree between what we morally expect of an adult human and of an adult chimpanzee.

It seems that moral awareness and moral responsibility is what makes us treat some animals with special respect. Probably this is what the Bible means when it says that humans are "made in the image of God" (Genesis 1:26). God knows the difference between right and wrong, and intentionally aims at what is right and good. Humans too know the difference between right and wrong, and should aim at the good. The difference is that humans are capable of knowingly choosing the bad, usually for self-centred reasons.

Potatoes certainly do not know the difference between right and wrong. I doubt whether ants do either. Cats and dogs? I doubt it. Chimps? To some extent, probably. Humans? Yes. Could there be other life-forms that know that difference? Certainly. So, we should not just talk about human beings. We ought to say that persons are special, because "persons" are beings that know the difference between right and wrong and know they ought to choose the good. There might be many sorts of persons in the universe, from little green men to intelligent lizards, perhaps. We can be sure that humans are persons, and that is what some people put misleadingly by saying that "only humans have souls." What they should be saying is that persons have some special qualities that distinguish them from almost all other animals on earth.

Persons can work out what is good, they can think about the future, and they can make plans to achieve good things in the future. When they do this, they are in fact working out what God's plan for their bit of the universe is. They are working out how they might help to achieve that plan. They can also make their own small but important creative contribution to the plan. Persons, unlike non-personal animals, are able to think about God's future plans. They are able to help achieve those plans by putting in their unique creative contribution. Persons are co-creators, "fellow-workers," the Bible says, with God (1 Corinthians 3:9).

Persons, in other words, make a positive contribution to the evolutionary process. They are able to understand how things work, and begin to change nature, to improve it so that they can move faster by having cars and planes, and heal better by using drugs and surgical operations. Regrettably, humans have also managed to use their understanding of nature to make bombs and destroy the environment. It seems that every positive possibility has its downside. But at least humans might be able to do something about that. Maybe a firmer belief that a positive and good future is possible and that it is the human task to bring it about can help humans out. I think that some form of belief in God is the best way to support such an optimistic outlook. However that may be, on this planet, humans are the only animals that can work out the laws of nature and use them to improve their lives and the lives of all living beings, so far as possible. We call that "science," and, supplemented by ethical commitment, it has improved the lives of humans enormously over the last few hundred years. This is a huge evolutionary advance.

Humans are the only animals on earth to write symphonies, mold sculptures, and write poetry. In doing this, they are using similar personal abilities, of understanding the materials they are working with—sounds, stones, and words—and using their creative imaginations to weave them into intricate and beautiful patterns. You may think that some modern art, like a urinal or an unmade bed, is not very beautiful. But when it is a work of art, you can sell a urinal for an enormous sum of money, even though it doesn't work. That takes some imagination, and no chimpanzee would ever have thought of doing it.

Humans are also the only animals on earth, as far as we know, to create stories about a spiritual dimension to existence, to tell stories of gods, and to try to relate to the source of their existence, sometimes (as in this book) imagined as a cosmic supermind, a planner of the story of the universe, a planner with which they may able to co-operate and to which they can relate in worship and prayer.

In short, human beings are persons because they have critical and reflective understanding (they can know what is right and wrong, what is true and false). They have creative freedom consciously to shape the future towards the goods of beauty, truth, and goodness or well-being. They are not special because they have an extra bit that other animals do not have. But they do have special abilities, which makes them persons. These abilities do not really have to involve solving differential equations and doing moral philosophy. There is no intelligence test you have to take before you can be a person. All you have to do is know the difference between right and wrong, and make a few moral decisions about how you are going to live. If I am right, being a person also makes it possible to have a conscious relationship to the mind of the cosmos, in other words, to be able to have a sense of the presence of God.

Of course, God cares about animals and about the life of our planet. On an evolutionary view of the cosmos, the cosmos develops from the Big Bang to form stars and planets, from single-cell life forms to complex organisms with consciousness and will. Persons are stages in the evolution of the cosmos. They are special because they are parts of the cosmos through which it can become aware of its nature and destiny, and who can help it to achieve that destiny. To put this in religious language, persons are able to discern God's will and obey it. They are able to do that. Whether or not they actually do it is another thing altogether. In fact, if they did it, we would not be in the mess we are in today.

My idea of God has changed quite a lot from the fundamentalist image of an all-controlling supernatural person who created the universe not very long ago, with human beings as the most important things in it, and the earth at the center of it, and who made everything in the universe just for the sake of men and women.

Modern science tells us about the immense size and age of the universe, and how the universe has developed from the simplicity of the Big Bang through billions of years of cosmic evolution to the complex and beautiful universe we inhabit today. This is a picture of the universe as gradually unfolding what was always embryonic in it, and humans are just a small part of that evolutionary process, not its center, nor its culmination.

It is not just human beings, it is the whole universe from the beginning that is of great beauty and awesome power and that has immense value just for its own sake. I came to see God as a supreme consciousness that carries these possibilities within itself, that sets the goals of great value, which the universe is intended to realize, and that in an important sense realizes its own nature as the universe gradually unfolds the possibilities that necessarily lie in the divine nature. This is a long way from fundamentalism, but I think it brings out more clearly what the creator (in whom the writers of the Bible definitely came to believe) of a universe like this (which the writers of the Bible did not really know much about) must be.

# CHAPTER THREE

# *Holding Infinity in the Palm of Your Hand*

## PLAYING SUPERCHESS

THIS BRINGS ME, STRANGE as it may seem, on to the second part of the Nicene Creed, which says that Christ is the "only-begotten" of God (in the 1662 Prayer Book English translation), and that he is "of the same substance as the Father." When we talk about Christ in this way, we are not talking just about the human being Jesus. We are trying to stand outside human history, and think about the eternal thought of God, or what we might call the divine Intellect. My own personal view is that the phrase "only-begotten" is very misleading. It almost inevitably makes you think that God had a son and so he must have had a wife. It has even suggested to some that Mary was the wife of God, which is really getting into polytheism in a big way!

In my opinion, what the word "only-begotten" (the Greek is *monogenes,* which can mean "unique" or "one of a kind") is trying to say is that God did not "make" Christ out of something else. Father and Son are two aspects of the one being of God. I think that makes sense. "The Father" is that aspect of the cosmic mind that is the source of all beings, and is beyond full human comprehension. It has knowledge and will, but in forms that are quite inconceivable to our limited minds. We cannot imagine what it is like to know every possible thing, or to be able to create a universe as vast and complex as this one. This is a mind far beyond any human mind. "The Son" or "the Word" or "the Christ" is the very same cosmic mind, but now as an intelligence that conceives of a specific universe, and makes that conception the goal of the cosmic process. The Son is God conceiving the plan of a universe, maybe of many universes.

The real problems start when the Creed says that the Christ "came down, took flesh, and was made human." To many people, this is a simple contradiction. How can the cosmic mind, which plans and sustains galaxies and stars, become a human being, a small primate crawling around on a small planet circling a small star in a small galaxy?

*Nobody* seriously thinks that Christ literally descended from heaven on a sort of spiritual escalator. Heaven is not up above. Christ, the eternal Word of God, always existed in the spiritual world. The claim is that this spiritual reality also took human form in this physical world. Just as the author of a play can become an actor in her own play, so the cosmic mind can appear as a finite thing in the cosmos it has created. It will still be the cosmic mind, with immense knowledge and power. But it can play a role in the game of life, and it could agree that the role it played could be limited by the powers allowed by the rules of the game.

Think of something like a computer game, where the designer of the game has an avatar or character within the game, which has to go through the same tasks and gain the same powers in the way that all the other characters do. The designer's character has a good chance of winning, since the designer made the rules up and knows exactly what they are and how to make the most of them. But that is not necessarily so, and the rules might even require all characters to die in various ways. That will, of course, make the game very annoying. The designer will not die, but his character might well die in the game. I doubt if any designer would let that be the last word.

Could we go a step further, and make a character have thoughts and feelings of its own, and make its own creative decisions? That would be a very complicated game, when the characters could make decisions that the designer did not like. The characters could get out of hand. If chess was like that, when one player tries to move a Bishop to a certain square, the Bishop might decide to go somewhere else instead. In a game of superchess, the rules might allow that, so the players would not have total control. They would set out the design of the game, so they would know that the choices the pieces can make will be limited. The players would have to build a set of probable but unpredictable moves into their calculations, so the game would get much more difficult. But it could be done.

In superchess, you could have many players, each with their own avatar. But in the game of life, there is only one designer. The characters, whose powers have been created by that designer, can make their own decisions within limits, governed only by the general rules of the game.

The designer can still make the rules so that the final outcome can be predicted, and can even influence the game to a certain extent, so that things do not get completely out of control. One way this can be done is to create some special characters who have a better grasp of the plans of the designer, special motivations to follow those plans, and special powers to be able to realize them.

There is no doubt that even though God does not create the eternal Christ, since it is the thought of God, God creates the human being Jesus of Nazareth. Jesus' thoughts, feelings, and powers are created by God. Jesus could be made uniquely aware of the presence and nature of the designer, could be uniquely inspired to desire and love the designer, and be uniquely empowered to follow the designer's plans, despite natural temptations to act as the other characters do, and ignore the designer's plans as much as possible.

Jesus could be a uniquely well-designed human character in the game of life. He would have his own thoughts, largely produced in the normal way through sense-perceptions and human teaching. But he would also have direct and intense mental awareness of the presence of God. Jesus would have his own feelings, tempered by his general experience of life. But he would also have a natural and intense love for God, and a sense of intimate relationship with God. Jesus would make many creative decisions of his own. But he would also have no inclination to frustrate or ignore the divine will for his life. That divine will would not need to cover every detail of Jesus' life, and it might be confined for the most part to a set of more general directives—like "heal people" or "Tell people about the kingdom of God."

This Jesus looks as though he would certainly be a super-saint. But could he be God, or the eternal Christ? Christian theologians have agonized and argued about this for 2,000 years, and they still do. What more would be needed, to turn a super-saint into God? We might say that we would never worship a super-saint, but we do worship God. There is the difference.

Why, however, would we never worship a super-saint? People have, after all, worshipped all sorts of things. They have worshipped stars, mountains, Roman Emperors, superheroes—there is even a tribe in the South Pacific that worships Prince Philip. We know that is called "idolatry" by people who do not like it. But what is really wrong with idolatry? Does it lead to immoral practices?

When I was president of an organization called the World Congress of Faiths I once said, "People of all faiths are welcome to join us." Then along came a young man who said, "I would like to join. I am delighted to find such a tolerant society. By the way, I am a Satanist."

I must admit I told the young man he could not join. Tolerance has its limits. But why was I against Satanists, or at least Satanists like him? I suppose it was because I thought it might be dangerous for young virgins, who tend to get sacrificed on moonlit nights. And because what many Satanists want is money, power, and sex, and I don't approve of those—at least, not in very large quantities.

In other words, what you worship must be good. It must be very very good. That is what was wrong with Roman Emperors and even, with all due respect, Prince Philip. They are not extremely good. That is also what is wrong with the Greek and Roman gods, who always seem to be eating their children or having sex with various animals. And it is probably what was thought to be wrong with the Canaanite gods of the Old Testament. They were thought to encourage bestiality, child sacrifice, and the search for power at any price.

A God who is worthy of worship must be so good that it could never conceivably be evil. It must also have enough power to be able to make good win the battle against evil. There is not much point in being good if you never actually get around to doing anything. A worship-worthy God would have some power for good with which we could align ourselves, to help us to be good. (Even if we are tempted to pray, with St. Augustine, "Lord, make me pure . . . but not yet.")

Perhaps it could have so much power and wisdom that we would be awe-struck at the scope of its abilities and the intricacy of its designs. Maybe it would be politic to fear such a God, and offer it food or sacrifices to keep it happy. But you would probably only worship it if it was really good. And if it was really good, it would almost certainly not be greatly impressed by being offered dead animals.

Worship is, when you think about it, very odd. It seems to be either offering dead animals to a God who does not need them, or telling God how wonderful and great he is, which God presumably knows already. Either way, it is pretty much a waste of time. So why do it?

We have to think again about worship. Try thinking of worship as acknowledging and expressing our natural reaction to meeting a being of supreme goodness, power, and wisdom. Worship is just the natural expression of attraction, admiration, and awe. It is not like flattering some dictator by saying, "I think you are wonderful. How wonderful you are. You are the most wonderful thing ever. I cannot stop letting you know about how I constantly wonder at your wonderfulness. By the way, just in case I was unclear, you really are wonderful." Worship is like being overcome by a sense we get of immense power, wisdom, and love, so that we cannot help loving and being in awe of what we see. It is just the immediate and natural response to a vision of supreme goodness, beauty, and creative power, in other words, to a vision of God.

## CUCUMBERS, BREAD, AND WINE

We probably have to admit, however, that we do not see God very clearly or very often. We need aids to worship, something that will remind us of the divine, or that will manifest the divine in forms we can understand.

There could be many forms that do this. Within Christianity people seem to worship God under the forms of bread and wine. To an outsider, it must seem very strange indeed that people are worshipping pieces of bread. It might make more sense to worship wine, but that is only if you like wine a lot.

Of course, people do not worship the bread and wine *as bread and wine*. Christians differ a lot about what exactly is going on in the central rite of most churches, variously called "the Lord's Supper" or "the Mass" or "the Holy Eucharist" or "Holy Communion." Many Protestants would object that bread and wine are not worshipped in *any* sense. They would mostly, however, think that Jesus is especially present during such a rite, and that Jesus is to be worshipped. More Catholic-minded Christians think that somehow Jesus is worshipped as fully present in consecrated bread and wine, but this remains a great mystery. The traditional Roman Catholic way of putting it is to say that the bread and wine continue to look and taste and feel like bread and wine, but their "substance," that which possesses all these sensory properties, is changed into something else—the body and blood of Christ.

I do not in any way want to downplay the significance of the Mass, but I have a problem here. My problem with this way of putting it is that I do not think there actually are any substances that can change all their observable properties and still be the same substances, or any things that can keep all their properties while changing their underlying substance. I belong to a philosophical tradition that says that substances just are sets of properties. There is no underlying thing that "holds them together." The nearest thing to a substance is the human self, which does possess experiences, and so is different from them, and which continues to exist through time as one and the same the same agent. Even this idea of a continuing self is very controversial among philosophers.

Even on a "continuing self" view, it would be odd to think that all the memories, thoughts, and feelings could remain the same, while the self changed into somebody else. Then I could wake up one morning, and say to my wife, "Hello, dear, I love you just as much as I did last night, and I remember the lovely supper we had, but unfortunately I have to tell you I have changed into a different person."

"How is that, dear?"

"Well, all my desires and memories are still the same. But actually it was not me who loved you last night, but somebody else with the same desires and memories as me."

"That is very interesting, dear. Who else was it?"

"Well it was somebody with the same name, the same address, and the same bodily odors."

"It sounds to me just like you, dear."

"That's the tragic thing. It was just like me, but it wasn't me. You see, it was my underlying substance that changed, so I really am a different person."

"But do you really still love me?"

"Well, somebody does, and that somebody is me. Somebody loved you yesterday, but that wasn't me. Or it was then, but it isn't any more."

"Has this ever happened before, dear?"

"I fear that it could be happening all the time. My self could be changing every day, or even every hour, and I would never really know. I would never know, because I might be a different person than I was when I started to ask if I was the same person."

"Do you know, dear, I don't mind who your underlying substance is, as long as it thinks and acts like the one just before it."

"But don't you realize you might be talking to somebody else?"

"Very well dear. But would one of you still like a coffee?"

I think the only way out of this conversation is to say that a continuing self is defined by its experiences and actions. A self can't pass on its experiences and actions to somebody else. In the same way, even if there are substances (which I doubt), they are defined by their properties, and they cannot just swap over at will, or whenever somebody says some magic words.

If that is the case, when Jesus says of a piece of bread, "This is my body," even he is not able to change the underlying substance into that which normally underlies a body, but now underlies a piece of bread. To make matters worse, it would be his own body that was now in the piece of bread, so he would be in two places at once, and he would be eating himself. Substances just cannot be interchanged, not even by God. If the properties remain the same, then the substance remains the same, whether or not there is any substance there at all.

Anyway, it still seems to me a form of cannibalism to eat another person's body, even if what you think you are eating is not really their body, but the underlying substance of their body. It would be better to do as some Pacific tribes do, and worship a cucumber. At least eating cucumbers would not be cannibalism. When they eat cucumbers in a special ceremony, they can say they are "eating God." If underlying substances can be swapped around, then they could be right. The properties of the cucumber remain cucumberish, but the underlying substance could be that of a potato, or God, or even of my aunt Agatha.

I believe that Christians do not really want to eat another person's body, even the underlying substance of another person's body. What they want, when they share in the service of Holy Communion, is to have the divine life, which was in Jesus, within them. They do not want it somewhere in their physical bodies, not even in the underlying substance of their bodies. The divine life must be a spiritual reality; it must be a mental power, with causal effects that enrich their mental lives or powers in some way. It is not physical at all.

What Roman Catholics are trying to preserve (in my opinion) is a sense that physical things can be conveyors of real spiritual powers. Substances are not spiritual powers, they are supposed to be hidden bits of physical things, which physicists, who specialize in physical things, amazingly do not know about. That is what I think is wrong with the Roman Catholic account. The physical might convey spiritual power, right enough. But it is not the same thing as that spiritual power. The question is, what are the spiritual powers, and how do physical things convey them?

Try this: spiritual powers are the gifts and fruits of the Spirit. They are mental qualities in finite spirits that are evoked by the actions of the

Supreme Spirit. They are relational, lying in the relation of Spirit to spirit. Something of the joy, wisdom, and love of Spirit is conveyed to a finite spirit. This is (believed to be) a real transaction, requiring the co-operation of Spirit and spirit, a deep relation of minds.

It seems to me perfectly reasonable to say that if there is a Supreme Spirit, it will be able to and will wish to convey some of its powers to created spirits. Since created spirits are embodied in a physical world, it would be appropriate for this to take place by means of a physical medium (just as finite minds normally, though not solely, communicate by opening their physical mouths and speaking).

I do not see why a cucumber might not be a physical medium for conveying spiritual powers. But I do not suppose that eating cucumbers will automatically give you advanced spiritual powers. Otherwise we might suppose that vegetarians will be more spiritually advanced than meat-eaters, and people who eat cucumbers will be more spiritually advanced than people who eat bananas.

Of course, you have to have a special relationship with cucumbers to receive spiritual powers from them. Probably, there must be some reason to think that cucumbers are especially appropriate expressions of Spirit, and that attending to cucumbers in the right way will be able to extract these expressions and inject them into the minds of cucumber worshippers. An appropriate way of such extraction and injection would be to eat them.

At the Feast of the Holy Cucumber, a particularly fine cucumber might be exhibited in a prominent place, and a story would be told of how and why the cucumber came to be a manifestation of Spirit. Maybe a cucumber saved a revered ancestor from starvation, thereby becoming the Cucumber of God that delivers humans from the wilderness and dangers of the desert of this world. The special thing about cucumbers is that they, by divine grace, can still convey spiritual powers that deliver believers from the deserts of despair. If they are eaten in a solemn way, hoping for the grace of the holy cucumber, then indeed spiritual power may be conveyed. A hymn may be sung to "the Cucumber of God, which takes away the sins of the world," and coffee and biscuits can be offered to everyone present after the service, to which all are invited, whether they really believe in cucumbers or not.

It may seem odd, even irreverent, to think of cucumbers in this way. But when the Christian gospel was taken to the Inuit inhabitants above the Arctic Circle, the first missionaries found great difficulty in convincing their hearers that Jesus was the "Lamb of God," since the Inuit had no great feeling for sheep, and most of them had never seen a sheep. They found that talking of Jesus as "the Penguin of God" had a much greater appeal. Penguins could be seen as manifestations of Spirit, and eating them with suitable devotion was a real help in protecting people against the cold as well as giving them an inner spiritual relation to what they might have called "Our Heavenly (or spiritual) Penguin."

Turning from cucumbers and penguins to Jesus, it may be that when he said, "This is my body" of a piece of bread, he was first of all referring to his own person insofar as it was a mediator of the spiritual presence and power of God, not just insofar as it was a physical substance. Then he was saying that the presence and power that was present in his life could be thought of as "spiritual food" that could bring life and health to his disciples. The "body" is the continuing spiritual presence of the risen Christ. Just as physical bodies make persons present to others, so bread, thought of as given by Jesus in a communal meal, can make the risen Christ present in a special way to those who have eyes to see or hearts to receive.

Jesus' actions at the Last Supper gave bread a special spiritual significance. If eaten reverently, it could convey the spiritual power of Jesus' life to devotees. As future generations of disciples eat the bread, in the context of thinking about communing with the risen Christ and remembering his self-sacrificial death by crucifixion, he will be spiritually present with them to empower them with his spirit.

In a similar way, wine conveys the spiritual power of life and self-giving love. When thinking of wine as "blood" we should recall that in the Old Testament sacrifices the blood of an animal was thought of as the life of the animal (Leviticus 17:11). So, in the Lord's Supper the blood of Christ means the risen *life* of and *spiritual power* of Christ. Bread and wine together convey the spiritual power of presence, self-giving love, and new life, which the life of Jesus manifested in a uniquely powerful way.

## WHY JESUS IS BETTER THAN A CUCUMBER

All this can be conveyed without getting into talk of substances changing while properties remain the same, which is a philosophical theory, not a biblical truth. Yet, it may be said, I may seem to have reduced the central rite of Christianity to the status of worshipping cucumbers or penguins. I am indeed suggesting that the crucial process of making a finite thing a vehicle of spiritual power is much the same in these, and many other, cases.

51

What matters in the end, however, is what the spiritual power is, and what it brings about in the lives of devotees.

I am not sure what cucumbers tell us about the ultimate nature of reality, and what special gifts they may bring us. In Jesus' case, the spiritual power is God's unlimited love, and what it brings about in devotees is a sharing in that divine wisdom and love. In the life of Jesus we see healing power, wisdom to understand the minds of others, and love for the poor of the earth. These qualities are just about as great as humans can manage, and they can evoke awe, admiration, and love in us, and make us Jesus' disciples.

Yet Jesus was not omnipotent and omniscient. Jesus, like the rest of us, had a rather small brain. The amount of information in that brain is strictly limited. It could not include knowledge of everything in the whole cosmos, including the theory of relativity and all the equations of quantum mechanics. There is just not room in one human brain for all that sort of stuff.

Also, if Jesus was really human, he could not do things like create new galaxies or universes. Jesus might well have had amazing power, wisdom, and love, but they would not be unlimited. So, should we really worship him, or just admire him as an outstanding saint? We might go so far as to say that if the love, power, and wisdom of God was going to be expressed in human form, this is as good as it could get. But, as a human being, he still would not have all the qualities of God.

However, when Christians say "the Word became flesh," they do not mean that the supreme God turned into a human person. They are trying to find a way of saying that the cosmic mind can be manifested in a human person, as fully as it can possibly be. The universal Spirit can use a human in order to act in the world. A human will do the job better than a cucumber, if only because humans are in a better position to demonstrate the nature of self-giving and unlimited love than cucumbers.

God can manifest the divine nature by means of a human person, rather as a superchess player can use an avatar to act within the rules of a computer game. Remember this is superchess, so the avatar, or game character, has a mind and will of its own. That mind can make its own creative decisions, and gains its knowledge through the senses, as all created minds (all the ones we know about, anyway) do. Yet it is used by the player to do the things that the player wants it to do. The character is not just a puppet whose every move is controlled by the player. It makes its own decisions, but the player ensures that all those decisions will be in line with what the player wants done, but that only a character can do.

There are two main things the player needs a character to do. One of these things is to manifest what God is in a way that humans (the other characters in the game) can understand. Since God is a mind who wills well-being for and responsive relationship with created persons, the most adequate manifestation of God will be a person who exemplifies such compassionate responsiveness. Since God is essentially creative and capable of personal relationship, the divine manifestation will be uniquely creative and loving. Union with God will not restrict creativity and free response; it will expand it, while always keeping in aligned with the general divine purpose.

The other main thing the player wants a character to do is to mediate to others the possibility of a unity of divinity and humanity, to reconcile humans, whose lives have moved far away from what God wills, back to awareness and love of the divine, to be filled with the power of the divine Spirit.

So it is that Jesus was, in the Christian view, not just an outstandingly good human being. He is also a manifestation of the nature of God and a human mediator of the presence and nature of God. Because that is so, we can worship the divinity mediated by Jesus in and through this human person, just as we can worship the divinity mediated in and through bread and wine, when they are taken to re-present, to make present, the life and work of Jesus.

If the Word of God adds a human person to itself, when that person acts it is not that God really does everything and the human person does nothing. God empowers a person to act in creative and insightful ways. This empowering relationship of the Spirit, present in Jesus from the first moment of his life, and mediated through him to those who put their trust in him, is what makes him the "incarnation" of the Word of God.

In my rejection of substance-theology, am I opposing Roman Catholicism? I am most certainly not. I am opposing the philosophical terminology used in traditional Roman Catholic expositions of the Mass. I am suggesting that "trans-substantiation"—the idea that the substance changes while the properties remain the same—is not the most helpful idea. In this case, it is the word "substance" that causes the trouble. As Thomas Aquinas says, in Question 3, Article 5, of the first part of his great work, the *Summa Theologiae*, God is not a substance anyway, so to say that Jesus Christ is of one substance with the Father is to use the word "substance" in a totally new and unusual sense, whose meaning is completely undefined. That is not helpful. It makes it too easy to think that Jesus was an omnipotent and omniscient being walking around in Palestine and pretending to eat food and learn things from his parents and teachers, when he did not need to eat and knew everything anyway.

To say that the "substance" of bread and wine changes into the "substance" of Jesus' body and blood is using the word "substance" in a different way again. The spiritual reality of Jesus can be truly manifest in bread and wine, even if there is no unperceivable "substance" underlying the bread, and if people are not really eating the "substance" of Jesus' physical body, which does sound too close to cannibalism for comfort. It can still be said that God is truly present in the Mass, in the special way that God was present in the person of Jesus. We do not have to sign up to the peculiar philosophical idea of "substances" changing while all their properties remain the same, which I do not suppose even Jesus or St. Peter ever thought of.

I think it makes sense to say that Jesus as an admittedly extraordinary human being manifested and mediated the cosmic mind on planet earth. His relation to God was not accidental or temporary. It was willed by God and was a union of a proper human person with the cosmic mind that could not be broken or dissolved. It was in this sense that "the Word became flesh," and it is in this sense that we can worship Jesus as the true image of God in human form and as the one through whom God reconciles the world to the divine life. However, Jesus always points beyond himself to the mind-like creator of the universe, and it is this God alone, whom we see and sense in Jesus, that we truly worship. Anyway, that is how, at the moment, I can make sense of the whole thing.

Fundamentalists have never gone in for trans-substantiation, but they do think of Jesus as God. In my experience, they do not think much about Christ as a cosmic figure, even though the Bible clearly says that "in him [Christ] all things in heaven and earth were created" (Colossians 1:16). This means that Christ includes the whole universe, and so is much more than just the human Jesus. It was as I thought more about this, and also began to think that the Lord's Supper was much more than just our remembering of Jesus having a meal, that I began to think of Jesus as the human vehicle of the cosmic Christ, and of the communion as the making-present of a truly cosmic self-sacrificial love to believers throughout the ages. I began to see physical things in the universe as possible sacraments of the presence and power of God. Little by little, my view of God's "saving action" in the world was getting wider and less confined to just one little group of conservative Bible-believing Christians.

# CHAPTER FOUR

## Dealing with Evil

### DANGEROUS FIGS

IT MAY SEEM ODD that just one person is the means by which the world, and maybe even the whole universe, is united to God. How can one human life have such amazing cosmic effects? Well, put like that it is very odd indeed.

It is the cosmic mind we worship, though our worship may be focussed on a finite object that is taken to manifest it. So, it is the cosmic mind that reconciles the created world to the divine, though that reconciliation may be channelled through a finite object that is taken to mediate it.

If the whole universe is reconciled to God, it will not just be through the human manifestation and mediation that Christians believe has come to *homo sapiens* on this planet. It will not, in other words, be through the human Jesus, though it may be through some appropriate finite mediator of the same cosmic and eternal Word that was mediated to us in and through Jesus.

Why do humans need to be reconciled to God? Here we come to the topic of sin, which is much more interesting to most people than goodness. Sin does seem interesting, which is precisely the human problem. If you look at paintings on medieval church walls, or in art galleries, depicting heaven and hell, it must be admitted that pictures of heaven are very boring. You have a lot of dopey looking people standing around with their hands together and their eyes looking up at the sky. Some play harps, and others read Bibles, but they all look very static and, well, to be honest, just boring.

Conversations in heaven are not much better. "Hello Daphne, I love you so much."

"I love you too Anne."

"Isn't it nice to love each other so much?"

"It's lovely. I love it."

"Do tell me all the news."

"News? Daphne, there isn't any news. No earthquakes, no disasters, nobody running away with someone else's wife. No arguments. No family quarrels. Just everybody loving each other, as usual."

"That's so lovely."

"Yes, isn't it? What should we do next?"

"Let's sing a hymn"

"What a lovely idea."

"Yes, everything we do is lovely. Don't' we just love it?"

"How long will the hymn last?"

"Forever, of course."

"Oh, lovely. I can't wait."

"You'll just have to Daphne, because we have billions of years of lovely hymns ahead of us."

"How lovely."

So much for heaven. Hell, on the other hand, is very exciting. There are always new tortures to be devised, new sins to be discovered, and lots of exciting adventures to watch. The thing is, hell is not so exciting once you are actually in it, but it is certainly fascinating just to see all that goes on there. And that really is the essence of hell. We don't like it when we get there, but we can't resist just trying to get a glimpse of what it is like. We especially like seeing other people going to hell, and at last getting what they deserve. We usually tend to overlook the fact that if that is the sort of thing we like, we are well on the way to going there ourselves. Because hell is precisely the place people go to when they take pleasure in the suffering of others.

In the Bible, sin all started with Adam and Eve. Though Eve is supposed to have eaten an apple, there is actually nothing in the Bible about apples, but she ate some sort of fruit—I guess it was figs, because the leaves would come in useful later, for covering various naughty bits—that God told them not to eat. There is a slight problem about that, because the fruit was supposed to give those who ate it the knowledge of good and evil. Before you ate the fruit, you had no such knowledge. So even though God told them not to eat the fruit, poor Adam and Eve did not yet know what wrong was, so they did not know it was wrong to take no notice of God. So, it was really not their fault that they ate a fig.

It was all a bit of a mix up. The snake did not help either. It was not actually a snake at the time, since it had legs. What it was doing in the garden I have no idea. Presumably God had put it there, so God must have known what was coming. Anyway, the snake, or dragon as it then probably was, spoke to them, they ate this fig, and the first thing that happened was that they noticed they had no clothes on. This was such a terrible thing that God made some clothes for them, deprived the dragon of his legs, told Eve that she would have trouble giving birth, told Adam that he would have to work hard all his life, told them both that they would eventually die, and threw them out of the Garden of Eden.

It does seem a rather excessive punishment for eating a fig. If you think, as many Christians have done, that all the descendants of Adam and Eve would suffer the same consequences, and in addition after that would be sent to hell for ever, you may well begin to wonder if the punishment is not rather excessive for such a crime, and whether this God is really suited for the job. God appears to be mostly concerned that Adam and Eve, when they knew the difference between right and wrong, would be "like one of us" (Genesis 3:22)—which seems to imply that there are lots of gods, and that their ideas of right and wrong are so perverse that they should be ignored entirely.

It is pretty obvious that this is a wholly imaginative story, taking elements from a lot of Middle Eastern mythology that happened to be around at the time. It has its positive points—there is only one God, who creates all things and offers eternal life and friendship to humans. Humans have become estranged from God by grasping at knowledge before they were ready for it. These points were an improvement on some other current myths. But the story still portrays God in a rather judgmental, even vindictive, light, and to that extent it needs a lot of further improvements—which the later Hebrew prophets were to give it, it should be said.

Most Christian theologians have not taken this story literally, but some of them have an even worse story to tell, if such a thing is possible. St. Augustine, who had his own sexual problems, put much of the suffering in the world down not to figs, but to sex. He did not think that Adam and Eve had simply failed to notice that they were naked because they not yet eaten figs. He thought that when they noticed they had no clothes on they were overcome by sexual desire. Their life, between having babies and trying to find food, was liable to be one long sexual orgy (though they could hardly commit adultery or be unfaithful, however hard they tried, since there was nobody else around).

There was nothing wrong, apparently, with making babies. But it was very wrong to enjoy it. It is not surprising that Christians have not been very good at sex. Some have thought that couples should pray before having intercourse. Some have even thought that they should pray while having intercourse, and that they should avoid sensations of pleasure if at all possible. They should certainly not have sex just for pleasure. Sex is for producing babies, not for having fun, or even for expressing love.

Augustine thought that not only did Adam and Eve get punished for fig-eating. They were guilty, Augustine thought, for disobeying God. Not only that, all their descendants were to be held guilty of disobedience also, even before they had done anything. From this weird opinion comes the idea of "original sin." All humans are born in original sin and therefore have original guilt. Unless something drastic happens, everyone deserves to be punished for ever.

This must be one of the most immoral ideas people have ever thought up. How can you be guilty of something you haven't done yet? And why should you be punished for something some remote ancestor did? The only thing to do with the idea of original sin and original guilt is to drop it like a hot potato (or perhaps in this case like a hot fig). (The idea of original sin is not, by the way, in the Bible, and it is not accepted by the Eastern Orthodox churches.)

What the terrible idea is getting at in its clumsy way, however, is not so silly. There is something wrong with the world. If God is a powerful, wise, and good creator, we would expect any world God creates to be full of wise and happy and good people. Yet Buddhists seem to have it right when they say that human life is filled with suffering and illness. People die in horrible ways. Not only that, they kill each other in horrible ways. They do not seem to be wise and happy, and it would be a very naïve person who thought people were all good.

What "original sin" comes down to is that people are not fully aware of God, and they find it impossible to be good all the time. If we drop the term "original sin," we still need to speak of estrangement—estrangement is ignorance of the fact that our whole existence depends entirely on a Supreme

Spirit of great wisdom and love. Consequently, we are unable to co-operate with that Spirit in realizing goodness and happiness in the world.

Much traditional Christianity finds it difficult to explain how this has come about. Admittedly it is not because of eating figs. It is surely not a punishment for somebody else's fondness for figs. It is surely not a punishment at all.

## DOES GOD GROW?

To understand this, we need to get into some seriously challenging stuff. That is because sin and suffering are pretty serious subjects. You may think what I say is laughable, but it is not quite so funny, and it may seem a little bit abstract. But, as doctors tend to say, it won't last long. What we have to do is to think again about the nature of Spirit (when I say "Spirit" I mean God, of course, but I am trying to avoid making people think of that bearded old man in the sky), and we need to do so in the light of the relatively recent idea of cosmic evolution.

The idea of evolution—not just of life on earth, but the evolution of the whole universe from the Big Bang to conscious intelligent life—has changed the way we think about human existence. It should also, in my view, change the way we think about God. What I have to say here may seem new and shocking, but it is really quite compatible with Christian belief—at least in the way I interpret it. It fits very well into a modern scientific view of how things are. It is also a very interesting philosophical theory, which is very widely held by myself and a few friends.

We begin with the idea that Spirit is the source of everything that exists. It is also the source of everything that could possibly exist, every state of affairs that could possibly be. Imagine a complete set of all possible states existing in the mind of the Supreme Spirit. That set is not just dreamed up in an arbitrary way, as though it could have been quite different. It has to be what it is, because if anything is possible, it is always possible, and ultimately those possible states just have to be the way they are. God has no choice about what possible states exist in the divine mind. At that level, God has to be the way God is. There is no alternative. God does not choose the divine nature. It just is—at the level of possibility, things have to be the way they are. In the Bible, God says to Moses, "I am that I am" (Exodus 3:14), which perhaps means, "Mind your own business" or possibly "This is the way I am. I can't help it. Get over it."

Some of these possible states have to be actual. Nothing can exist if it is merely possible. One thing that has to be actual is Spirit itself, in which all possibilities exist. Suppose now, just as a thought-experiment, that Spirit is essentially creative and self-realizing. It develops its own nature by making some of its own potentialities actual. Think of Spirit as a dynamic power that is continually bringing possible states into existence. There is creative freedom in this process, but that freedom is limited by the nature of the potentialities that exist in the divine mind, and the connections that exist between them.

To help to envisage this, think of the way in which a baby grows. Babies have certain characters that, given the right circumstances, will develop in certain ways. One baby might have an inborn ability to play and write music. That ability will develop if there actually are things like pianos, orchestras, and music teachers around. The exact way it develops will be partly due to the creative choices the baby makes as it grows up. But babies are not free to be anything—great golfers, musicians, or scientists. There is a limited set of possibilities for a baby. As it grows, it will have limited freedom of choice. The limits are set by its inborn character and by the environment in which it grows.

At Christmas time, when baby Jesus is in the manger, Christians think of God as a baby. Maybe this is a more profound picture than it seems. It does not mean that God has tantrums and cries a lot at nights. But maybe it means that God gradually develops new possibilities in the universe as time goes on, and is constantly seeking new adventures and ideas.

If this is true, then the Supreme Spirit has a history. It has a process of self-development. This will involve free creativity, but it will be limited by its inherent nature and by the environment in which it works. It may seem strange to say that Spirit works in an environment that limits its choices. It is true that there will be no conditions independent of Spirit that form its environment. But now suppose that Spirit by its inherent nature creates an environment within which it develops.

This is because Spirit, at least as I am imagining it, is essentially relational. It does not just develop itself, as though it is content to be the only conscious intelligent being in existence. It seeks to develop its own nature by relation to other personal beings. So, it has to create some other beings, with which it can interact. The Christian tradition puts this by postulating that "God is love" (1 John 4:8), and love is a relation between persons by which they allow each other creative freedom to share actions and experiences. Spirit, as the ultimate cause of all things, retains its supremacy and primacy. But its own nature drives it to create other persons with whom it can realize that nature as love. Could it be that God would be less than perfect if God had nobody to talk to but God? If there was nothing but God, God could certainly spend the time admiring the divine perfection. But might that not be just a little bit self-centred? That might be inevitable, if there was nothing in existence but God. But it is not inevitable, because God can create somebody else to talk to—and, more importantly, somebody else to love.

The story of the created cosmos is an evolutionary story. Created things develop, as children do, by passing through stages from simple potentiality (in the case of children, a fertilized egg) through growing maturity (a usually rather annoying adolescence) to final full development. With human children, they often do not grow to maturity, and even if they do, they are bound to die sooner or later. With Spirit, growth to maturity is, presumably, assured, and Spirit does not die. Yet one can envisage the whole cosmic process as one of developing possibilities to their full flowering. Such development will involve both creative striving and resistance, as the new often confronts and overcomes the old, and reacts to changing conditions and competing visions. Spirit shares all the experiences of created persons, so Spirit itself will change and come to have new experiences, experiences that it would not have had if this creation had not existed.

Does God, then, evolve? Not, I suppose, in the way that a human baby evolves from ignorance to knowledge and from weakness to strength. Not even in the way that organic life evolves from simple cells to complex nervous systems and brains. God—Spirit—will always be the creative and relational source of all beings, and will possess the power, wisdom, and knowledge to guide the development of the cosmos. In other words, God is not the end point of a process of evolution that starts without any knowledge or power or wisdom. God has an eternal nature of maximal knowledge, power, and wisdom. This nature does not evolve. It will, however, be continually expressed in a developing cosmos that includes many emerging, creative, and relational persons. God will relate in creative and co-operative ways to entities within this cosmos, and will include everything in this and maybe many other universes within the divine being. In that sense God will grow. God will embrace an evolving creation in the divine being, but God will always remain one and the same Supreme Spirit.

If you have a theory like this, you will not think that God created human beings perfect in a beautiful garden fully equipped with figs. You will not think that humans were then ejected from the garden, and became guilty for disobeying God.

Instead, you will see the whole physical cosmos as beginning from a state of ultimate simplicity—just one point of huge energy, without consciousness, value, complexity, or structure. Then, beginning from the "Big Bang" at the start of our spacetime, it develops through stages of increasing complexity and structure, forming fields of energy, particles, atoms, molecules, organic life, nervous systems, and conscious brains. Patterns, values, and purposes emerge as the possibilities in the divine mind unfold themselves successively through all the grades of possible being.

Some scientists think this whole process is accidental, without purpose, and completely unpredictable. But believers in God think that the universe did not start just with an unconscious "Big Bang." What always existed was the Supreme Spirit itself, which thought of the universe and consciously decided to get it going and direct its course. I think that this is a much more likely explanation of the developing history of this incredibly complex and organized universe than saying it was just an unconscious accident. If you think Spirit is the source of all beings, the process will look more like one directed towards a goal of great value. That goal will be development of some of the possibilities in the mind of Spirit (this will be the cosmic Christ or *Logos*). God will realize those possibilities through creative interaction with a created community of personal minds. It is this creative interaction that makes it possible for God to be self-giving love (what the New Testament calls *agape*).

In the course of evolution, as fully conscious minds begin to exist, there is the possibility of conscious co-operation with Spirit, and of a growth towards creative and compassionate communities. Even then, there will be obstacles to be overcome, dangers to be avoided, and disasters to be endured. For these things are possibilities inherent in the cosmic mind, and they become existent as the evolutionary process moves through its various stages, often destroying the old and laboriously building the new. It is not that God positively intends them to exist. Even God cannot eliminate them. What God consciously intends is good, yet God God's will, even if ultimately victorious, is constrained by the necessities that exist in the divine being itself.

## LIVING IN SIN

In a universe where finite minds are creatively free not to co-operate with God or with their fellow creatures, this, whether inevitably or just as a matter of fact, leads to estrangement. Because of this, not everything that God wills comes to pass. Lots of things happen that God does not will. All things come from God, both good and bad. But not all things are *willed* by God. This may upset some people, who think that God's will must always be done, and that God can do anything God wants. I do not know how they know that. They seem to be committed to saying that if I do evil, that is what God wills, and it is hard to see why I should be blamed for doing what God wills—I know Calvinists disagree, but it is hard to see why! And this gives no explanation for the amount of evil and suffering in the world. Surely a good God cannot want that, and would eliminate it if God could.

The solution is clear. God *cannot* eliminate all suffering. So, we have to distinguish between what comes from God by *necessity*, and what comes from God by *conscious intention*. Such a distinction is possible—we are very familiar with the fact that in our own case sometimes we do what we want, and sometimes we do things we do not want to do. God might be in the same boat.

It may then be said that I am just making this idea of God up to suit myself. This is not quite fair. I got the idea of God from the Bible, but as you now know I do not take the Bible as infallible. I see in the Bible a long development of thinking about God, culminating (for me) in the idea that God is a universal creator who wants everyone to have a life of goodness and happiness. We still have to go on developing this idea of God, as our experience of Christ and of the world in which we live grows. Of course, the way we develop biblical ideas about God will be a very personal thing. But everyone's idea of God is a personal thing. It's just that mine is better than anyone else's (that was a joke, at last). I do think my idea gives a better account of the facts of suffering in the world than some others. And I do not think, incidentally, that the Bible gives a very clear view of the matter—God and the angels seem to fight with Satan and with Leviathan (see, for instance, Psalm 74:13 and Isaiah 27:1), so presumably they do not agree with what Satan and co. are doing. Or did God positively intend that Satan should fall from heaven and cause so much trouble? I would have thought that God was very displeased about the whole thing, which means that God did not want it to happen.

People naturally want God to be as good as possible. My account accepts this, but says that it is not possible for God, or for any being at all, to be able to do absolutely anything. God is as good as God can get. Maybe what really matters is that good will triumph in the end, and that we will be able to see some point in our sufferings—that is, see that such suffering, though it was never good, was a necessary part of a world that on the whole is and in the end will be good.

Some Christians have thought that death is a punishment for Adam's sin, and that suffering and death came into the world because of sin. That does not seem to me at all likely. Death existed in the animal world long before there were any humans, and even among humans the people who suffer are not very often the people who have sinned the most.

What does seem likely, however, is that human wrongdoing, hatred, greed, and egoism have made things a lot worse than they need to be. Human beings in general are very self-centred; they tend to dislike people who are different from themselves; and they quite like to treat other people as slaves if they can get away with it. Even a quick look around our world shows that people are not co-operating with a Spirit who wills that all people should show care for the well-being of others.

The philosopher John Stuart Mill was a great defender of utilitarianism—the view that we should aim at the greatest happiness of the greatest number. But he admitted that when he got to know a great number of other people, he found it hard to like them very much. As one of his friends said, "Why should I spend my time trying to make people I don't like, and usually disapprove of, as happy as possible? Just look at them!"

There might not have been an actual Adam and Eve in a garden. But there must have been a first person who felt that there was something they ought to do, and just could not be bothered. There was a choice between doing what is right and seeking pleasure for oneself. There were probably many people who had that sort of choice, many Adams and Eves. Whether it was inevitable that sooner or later they had to choose pleasure over obligation I do not know. But they actually did. And enough of them did so to create a society of self-seeking individuals who naturally starting arguing and competing with each other over scarce resources.

The theory of evolution actually gives a much better explanation of how sin arose than the book of Genesis does. That is not surprising, because Genesis does not try to give a scientific explanation. It is a story to make some points about the human situation in general. But in that story, there is no clue as to why God creates snakes and figs that are only going to get people into trouble.

On an evolutionary account, an important part of the story is that as animals evolve (as mutations occur in their DNA) the more lustful and aggressive animals are likely to survive and propagate offspring more successfully. Obviously having lots of sex and killing your competitors off is going to be good for the survival of your own genes. This is called "evolution by natural selection," though a better term might be "selection by ruthless elimination."

Christians would probably not want to say that this is the only evolutionary mechanism. They would stress that the laws of nature and the nature of the environment make the development of consciousness and intelligence likely, even though they are not strictly necessary for evolutionary dominance. Also, lust and aggression need to be complemented by care for offspring and co-operative behavior if they are to be most effective. The evolutionary story is not just one of repeated accidents and bad behavior.

Nevertheless, the "natural selection" story shows that lust and aggression are natural features of the biological process. What used to be called "the *fall* of humanity" (from the garden of Eden) can now be seen as more like "a *failure to rise*," to control inborn tendencies to lust and aggression and direct them towards love and cooperation.

When people failed to exert such control, when they knew they could do so and should do so but did not do so, sin began, and it did cause suffering. There is a connection between sin and suffering, though it is not the direct sort of connection that says: if you sin, you will die. On the contrary, the rule rather seems to be: if you sin, other people will die. One of the things wrong with any theory that says you suffer because you deserve it is that it is usually the innocent who suffer, because they are the ones who get trampled on by the greedy.

Humans have a problem. We are born into societies where greed and hatred are dominant. It is virtually impossible for anyone to escape these influences. The funny thing is that if you hate greed and hatred, you are beginning to hate something, and so logically you have to hate yourself (think about it; it's a valid argument!).

We don't need to believe in Adam, Eve, the garden of Eden, and talking snakes to believe that God has a plan for the world, and that humans have turned away from it, and therefore from God as well. Humans are estranged from God; they no longer know God's presence or are able to obey God's will. That is really what "being in sin" means.

## LOOKING FOR A GOOD RELIGION

The religions of the world are very largely ways of trying to come to terms with the problem of human estrangement. How can we know God better, and learn to obey God's will (they wouldn't all put it in that way, of course)? Put more generally, how can we become more aware of the presence of a Supreme Spirit (or, even more vaguely, of a spiritual dimension to life), and how can we align ourselves with the goals of the cosmos, escape from greed and hatred, and realize new and unique values in our lives and in the world around us?

I don't think there is only one possible way of doing this. There are many religions in the world, largely distinguished from one another by their funny hats. It is hard to overestimate the importance of hats in religion. Some religions force men to wear hats in places of worship; others forbid that. One early Christian, according to some interpreters of the New Testament, required women to wear hats in church, because otherwise he thought the angels could get over excited (1 Corinthians 11:10). Hair can be important too. Some religions advocate shaving all your hair off; others forbid you to cut your hair, or tell you to cut it in special ways. But hats are the most important thing. The shape of your hat is important. Only top Christians can wear pointy hats, and the more important you are the bigger your pointy hat will be.

In the Anglican Church, collars are also quite important. You can also tell what sort of minister you are by what you wear around your neck. If you wear a very wide white clerical collar you are very evangelical, and are always asking yourself what Jesus would do, and then telling other people what it is. If your collar is narrower, you are much more respectable, and hardly talk about Jesus at all. If you just have a speck of white collar showing in a generally black surround, you have dangerous Catholic tendencies, and are probably addicted to incense and other dangerous substances. If you do not wear a clerical collar at all, you have either forgotten what it is you believe, or you are making the point that you do not think that there should be any clergy, and therefore that you do not really exist.

Food is also an important matter for many. Hindus do not eat cows, Jews do not eat pigs, and English people do not eat dogs. No-one is quite sure why, but the rules can be very strict. I once had breakfast with a group of Orthodox Jewish Rabbis, and we were happily eating bagels, which were naturally Kosher bagels, and thus the Rabbis could happily enjoy them. But then one young and very keen Rabbi asked the question, "What oven were these bagels warmed up in?" Silence fell. But now the question had been asked, it had to be answered. "It was the oven that is used for cooking all breakfasts." 'Does that include ham and eggs?" 'Well, yes it does." "Especially ham?" 'Yes." The assembled Rabbis stopped eating at once. This oven had rendered even bagels unclean. At last one of them said, "Why on earth did you ask that question? We were enjoying our bagels. Now breakfast is ruined." Sometimes ignorance is bliss. Anglicans do not, of course, worry about bagels. But try getting them to eat dogs!

As well as questions about hats and food, there are some more abstract matters on which religions disagree, like whether there is a God or not, or whether your grandmother was a runner bean. This belief about grandmothers may seem an unlikely belief, but the ancient Greek thinker Pythagoras forbad his followers to eat beans, and one story goes that this was because he thought that beans might be reincarnations of people, and more particularly of his grandmother. I do not know what you need to have done to be reincarnated as a bean, but I assume it is nothing very good. I also wonder whether a bean knows it is a reincarnated person, who has been turn into a bean because of what it did when it was a human. If it does not know this, there does not seem much point in turning someone into a bean. After all, they will never know that they are beans, much less why they are. If it does know this, then beans are much more intelligent than we thought. Either way, I see problems in Pythagoras' view.

But that is the peculiar thing about religion. Everybody else's religion seems to be very silly, while one's own is obviously true. To many English people, refusing to eat bacon seems silly. But try getting the same people to eat fillet of dog, and they will be scandalized. Atheists often think it is silly to believe that a man walked on water, turned water into wine, and rose from the dead. But Christians think it is silly to think that intelligent beings came into existence completely by accident, and that consciousness does not even exist (which some atheists apparently say, though whether they say it consciously is not clear!).

When you look at all the different things that people think, most of them concluding that what other people think is silly, you quickly realize that there is no universally accepted test of silliness. There is no proof that your own view is not silly, either. Should that worry you? It should worry you a bit! It should at least make you think that your view, whatever it is, is not the only reasonable and obviously true one. And it should make you realize that various rules about pigs and hats are largely cultural matters that help to define communities of like-minded people, but are not worth getting very worked up about, seen in the light of eternity.

You cannot believe everything. So nobody can believe all religions, though I did find a "Church of All Religions" in California. I wonder if they included Satanists and Strict and Particular Baptists? Still, you have to believe something—even if you think all religions are silly, that is a belief, and it is pretty silly, since you couldn't possibly have come across all religions, so how do you know?

The place I myself would start from is with moral beliefs and ways of life. I am going to be rather dogmatic and say that almost everyone knows that we should be kind to others and that we should not kill innocent people on purpose. A good religious view will be one that supports such moral beliefs and roots them somehow in the reality of the universe.

Then I would suggest that a good religious view will accept the well-established finding of science, like the size and age of the universe and the fact of evolution. You don't have to accept all the interpretations of these findings, because scientists are usually just as silly as the rest of us. But it is unwise to have a belief that contradicts a pretty basic scientific finding.

I would also want a religion that was psychologically positive, building on experiences that extend and deepen one's sense of personal self-worth and purpose, that lead to a sense of sharing in a greater reality of wisdom and compassion, and do not lead to hatred of or indifference to others.

This is already enough to rule out a lot of religious views. It will probably not rule out religions as such. But it will, for instance, rule out Christian views that heretics should be burnt at the stake, or Muslim views that infidels should be stoned to death. It will probably rule out most forms of Satanism, though it is possible that there exist some kindly Satanists who just feel sorry for fallen angels and like dancing around naked in the moonlight.

These are tests for seeing how good your religious (or non-religious) view is. But the basic view you have is largely put in place by what you have been taught as a child, and perhaps by what you have liked or disliked. That is where you start from, and any halfway good Supreme Spirit will understand that, and not blame you for it.

If the Supreme Spirit takes my advice, it will be concerned for the well-being of all people of all faiths, and will actually do something to try to relate them positively to Spirit. What it will do will depend on the conditions and background traditions of various cultures, so there will be many ways of relating to Spirit. Christianity is just one of them. What I am interested in is forging a sort of faith that supports a sound morality, is consistent with modern science, is psychologically helpful, and has some sort of philosophical backing, however controversial it is. And I am looking for a religious view, if there is one, that deals with the problem of human estrangement in a plausible and effective way.

## WHY DID JESUS DIE?

For many people, the most important thing about Christianity is what it says about estrangement and how to cope with it. The Nicene Creed, which I am still talking about when I remember to do so, says that Jesus "came down from heaven for our salvation." I have pointed out that Jesus did not come down on an escalator. It was the eternal Wisdom of God that united uniquely with the human person of Jesus, from the very first moment of Jesus' existence. That person became the authentic manifestation and mediator of Spirit to this planet. While some saw him at first as the deliverer of Israel from Roman domination, he was more truly seen as the deliverer of all people from the domination of greed, pride, and hatred, from estrangement or "sin." Yet he died on the cross, as a criminal. So, the deliverance was not very obvious. What Christians came to say was that Jesus died for us, so that we could be liberated from sin and made one with God. This seems very odd to many people. How could one death accomplish such a thing?

There have been various ways of trying to explain this, none of them totally satisfactory. One way, the fundamentalist way, which was, to the surprise of most fundamentalists, largely invented by Protestants in the sixteenth century, is to say that all people are born in original sin, and are therefore guilty and deserve to die and go to hell for ever. The only way to escape this fate, to be "saved," is to believe that Jesus died on the cross. His death paid the price of our original sin, and only those who believe that will be saved from a fate worse than death.

Unfortunately, I think that almost everything is wrong with this account. I have already got rid of original sin and hell, so you do not need to be saved from them. I do not see how the death of a man on the cross could pay the price for anybody else's sin, let alone the sins of everybody who has ever been born. Even if it could, it does not seem right that a punishment due to a guilty person could be taken on board by a completely innocent person. However well-meaning, that just seems grossly unjust. Finally, why should just believing that such a thing had happened save me from all the punishment otherwise due to me? It seems weird to think that accepting a particular belief could turn me from a guilty person into an innocent one.

People who believe this sort of account will say I have given a very unfair description of it. Well, yes, in this book I am doing my best to be equally unfair to everybody, including myself. I actually do see the emotional appeal of thinking that I deserve to die, and Jesus has died in my place. It will certainly evoke great devotion for Jesus, and it may well renew my moral endeavours and change my life for the better. It may be important not to lose these things. On the other hand, it would be better if I could get them without having to accept such a very legalistic and judgmental story about what is supposed to be a loving God.

Let's start again. Humans do have a problem. The problem is that if there is a Supreme Spirit who desires a personal relation with humans and wishes to co-operate with them for good, we seem to be largely unaware of this. We do not feel the divine presence, and we seem unable to do the good things it wants us to do. We are stuck in egoism, hatred, and greed. This might not be hell, but it tends to be hell for other people, while they for their part seem to be doing their best to make life hell for us.

To deal with this problem, three main things seem to be needed. First, we need a stronger and more adequate sense of the presence of God. Second, we need power to overcome our egoism and hatred, power that can at least begin to turn our lives around and make them forces for good. Third, we need some hope that it is worth doing what is good, because good will triumph in the end, and our efforts will not just be in vain.

To put it in traditional Christian terms, we need faith—a vibrant personal relation with a God of supreme mercy and compassion; love—a concern for others that can outweigh our overbearing concern for ourselves; and hope—a conviction that all things in the end work for good.

These are things we need *now*. They are not beliefs about what happened to someone a long time ago, or about how we can find a way of avoiding some punishment that is hanging over us. So how has the death of Jesus on the cross anything to do with it?

The best way to start is to recall that the whole cosmos is the expression of Supreme Spirit. Yet not every part of the cosmos is an equally good expression. There are billions of light years of empty space (at least it seems empty to us). That is probably not a very good expression of Spirit, except that it may remind us that Spirit is very big. Human beings are better expressions, because they often have wisdom and intelligent creativity, and these are things that Spirit has.

Then again, some human beings are better expressions, are more Spirit-filled, than others. That is, they have a better idea of the nature of Spirit, they have a more vivid personal relation with Spirit, they seem able to live morally heroic lives, and they seem able to convey the power and presence of Spirit to others.

I would include figures like the Buddha, the prophet Muhammad, some Sikh Gurus, some Indian holy men and women, and Jesus in my list of the top ten Spirit-expressers. They express Spirit in different ways, and they have different ideas about exactly how men and women are to relate to Spirit. They cannot all be right in everything they say. But they are heroes of the Spirit, people of quite extraordinary spiritual gifts.

Such people can be called icons of the Spirit, parts of the cosmos who are able to manifest and mediate the nature, presence, and power of Spirit in outstanding ways. For Christians, Jesus is an iconic manifestation of Supreme Spirit as love. I am sorry about using the word "iconic." In these days of the hyper-inflation of adjectives, almost any can be described as iconic. The Taj Mahal is an iconic building; the winner of the BBC wedding-cake competition is described as having made an iconic wedding cake; and Marilyn Monroe was an iconic film star. Nevertheless, I can't think of a better word for what I want to say—which is that Jesus was a picture or model—an icon—of something else, something of great significance or value, but that we cannot adequately see or describe, and that we could not have seen at all without the existence of Jesus.

His whole life, his teachings, his healing power, his compassion and love, his death on the cross, his resurrection, his ascension, and his gift of the Spirit to his disciples—all these things taken together form one iconic presentation, one finite living model, of Supreme Spirit.

Jesus' death on the cross is only part of this totality, but it is a crucially important one. These days the image of the cross has largely lost its significance. I tried to buy a small cross in a local jeweller's shop, and the girl behind the counter said, "Do you want one with a little man on it?" Yet for those who know that Jesus is more than a little man on a cross, the cross has a profound meaning. It shows that the nature of Spirit is *self-sacrificial love*, and that *God shares to the full in human suffering and despair*. It is, however, of vital importance that the cross was not the end. Because Jesus was raised from death, this shows that divine love is stronger than death. That is, the power of God's love gave Jesus a continued existence in the spiritual world after his physical body had died. Christians think that God has the power to give us all such a continued existence, "eternal life." Disciples of Jesus throughout the world and throughout all ages can, by living a self-sacrificial life, "die to self," and be raised by God to a new life, which will continue beyond the death of their physical bodies.

Jesus' death was not just something that happened a long time ago, and at that particular date magically changed God's attitude from vengeful hatred to compassionate love. Jesus' death was an icon of eternal Spirit, a finite manifestation of what Spirit always and everywhere is. It is iconic for people today, because Spirit is always self-sacrificial love. It shares in our experiences of loss and pain, but it also promises that we shall live after physical death in the presence and knowledge of God.

In Christian churches, Jesus' sacrifice is ritually re-enacted as a sacrifice of bread and wine. This is a re-presentation, a making-present, of his iconic death and resurrection. It makes the divine love, which is eternal but which is held to be truly and authentically manifest on the cross, present and effective to those who attend to it. That is how the death of a man long ago can mediate a present transformation of life. Jesus' self-sacrifice and his rising to more glorious life is made present to us in bread and wine, whether it is called the Lord's Supper or the Holy Eucharist. This event makes God present in loving relation to us, it strengthens us to love and obey God's will for justice and compassion, and it fills us with hope that all things will ultimately be well.

Jesus sacrificed his life because of his loyalty to the divine will. This was not a magical transaction. It was not that the offering of his blood in some magical way persuaded an angry God, who wants blood, to forgive the sins of all humanity. I reject totally the idea that God requires an offering of blood to pay for sins. I do not think sins can be "paid for." If you steal ten pounds (or even ten dollars), you can pay off your crime by returning the money plus interest. But if you murder someone, there is no way you can return them to life. You can be punished by being sent to prison, but how much prison "pays for" a murder? That just doesn't make sense.

It is a primitive view of punishment that thinks of it as "paying for" crime. "Let the punishment fit the crime," went the Gilbert and Sullivan song. But what punishment fits the crime of rape? Or what punishment fits the crime of torturing a child? True, we feel people shouldn't just get away with doing terrible things. But what would somebody who really cared for the ultimate well-being of everyone do? It is a puzzle!

Some crimes can never be undone. Killing millions of innocent people cannot be undone. Even the death of a man or even of a God on the cross cannot undo such things. Persons who do such things have made themselves persons who have contempt for others, who are unable to love, who are enslaved by their own hatred and destructiveness. Perhaps the only just punishment is to let them be themselves, in the company of others like them, and experience the spiritual desolation and emptiness that they have made for themselves.

What they have done cannot be undone. But what they have made of themselves can be unmade. That is what a loving God would do, help them to unmake the persons they are, and to become members of a truly loving and compassionate community.

That is the theory behind imprisonment in the UK and in America, believe it or not. It is partly to prevent crime. But it is also, and in theory primarily, the attempt to reform criminal minds. In British prisons it does not seem to work very well, though it is not impossible. God has more time and patience, but even for God it may be an uphill battle. What Jesus' death on the cross shows is not that God will save a few chosen people from eternal damnation if they "are washed in the blood of the Lamb," which sounds a fairly gruesome way of having a bath, but that God will go to any lengths to reconcile estranged humans to the divine, including experiencing suffering and death. It is not the death that saves. It is *the risen life and power* that saves. But this could not be known as the power it is without a death and resurrection.

Jesus' death shows that God shares in the suffering of the innocent. Jesus is crucified, not because God wanted him to die, as a payment that God required but decided to pay in person. Jesus died because that is what happens to a good person in a world of fear and hatred. Since God knew that would happen, in that sense God willed Jesus to die, but it was *God* who died, not somebody else. God was thereby able to show that death could be defeated by love, for physical death was not the end, and love endures forever. Jesus' death and resurrection shows that God will bring human lives to fulfilment, despite all their sufferings. That is what Christians call atonement, being made one with God.

It is with belief in original sin and substitutionary atonement (that Jesus' death was the punishment that God requires to pay for my sin) that I most clearly broke with fundamentalism. I just don't believe these things. I do believe that humans are estranged from God, and that this largely results from the selfish choices of our remote ancestors. I do believe that Jesus' death was the result of human sin, and that his risen life re-unites us to the divine life. But I simply cannot accept any account of this that turns God into a vindictive judge who is happy to let someone else take my punishment, as long as someone gets punished. Luckily, the Bible does not have to be interpreted in these ways, and its major teaching, which the death of Jesus shows, is that God is a God of unlimited and self-giving love for everyone without exception. That is the gospel I came to accept.

# CHAPTER FIVE

## *What Do We Know about Jesus?*

### WHERE DID JESUS GO?

WE DO NOT WANT to say that religious faith is just a belief that some funny things happened a long time ago. On the other hand, what happened in the past has sometimes had important effects on how we live now. Isaac Newton discovered gravity, and that knowledge has changed the world. Beethoven wrote music, and it can change or improve people's lives when they hear it today.

So, it might be important that Jesus started a spiritual movement that still has effects on many people today, for better or worse. Christian churches, in all their variety, certainly affect people today. Where would we be without jumble sales, crazy vicars, Cathedral choirs, and white weddings? Whatever we think about that, the world would certainly be a different place without churches.

So, is Jesus somebody who started a church? Well, I don't suppose he gave Peter a pointy hat and silver slippers, and said, "You are the first pope and you are infallible. Appoint some cardinals at once and start saying Mass in Latin." I should think Christian churches really started with meetings in small rooms in Jerusalem, when a group of people suddenly started singing and waving their hands in the air. These people had been followers of the man Jesus, thinking that he was the Messiah, someone who would liberate Israel from Roman domination and usher in a new Golden Age. This much at least is as certain as almost any other fact of ancient history.

Jesus (not his real name, which was Joshua) was a man, not a myth. But he was a very puzzling man, who had called people to follow him, but who had annoyed all the religious authorities and had eventually been put to death as an alleged claimant to be the real King of Israel (though he didn't seem to be in favor of armed insurrection). You might have expected that his disciples would give up and go back home. But they kept on going to the temple and praying, and there were claims that even though he was dead he had appeared to groups of them, who claimed that he had been raised to the presence of God, where he really was King.

This was much more fishy. Half the Jews did not believe there was any life after death, and the other half thought that there might be, but the dead were asleep until the Last Judgment, when they would all simultaneously wake up. For the latter group there was life after death, but it had not happened yet, at least in a very satisfactory form. There can be little doubt, however, that some disciples *thought* they had seen Jesus (or, in Paul's case, a vision of the risen Jesus), something that convinced them he was not dead after all.

These experiences were so odd that it was hard to describe them in straightforward terms. I remember Michael Ramsey, Archbishop of Canterbury, giving a lecture on the resurrection appearances of Jesus, which concluded with the statement that "We cannot be sure exactly what the resurrection was, but whatever it was, I certainly believe it."

The resurrection can sound very odd indeed, if you think that we are just animals, and that when our brains stop working, we will simply have ceased to exist, end of story. It is a very common thought, these days, that consciousness is nothing more than a function of the brain. You cannot be conscious, they say, if you have no brain, so it is actually impossible to go on thinking if you have lost your brain.

Admittedly it is very hard to prove this, either way. It looks as though if you damage the brain, your consciousness gets affected, and that might make you think that if you destroy the brain, consciousness just stops. On the other hand, it is very easy to imagine that my body, including my brain, could disappear, and I could just go on thinking, feeling, and even seeing. Science fiction stories are full of such imaginations. They do not seem to be impossible. It seems to be the case that under normal conditions consciousness is causally dependent upon the correct functioning of the brain. However, it is obvious that if one thing causes another then those two things could exist apart. You could get all the neurons of the brain firing, without any conscious experiences occurring. And you could have lots of conscious experiences without any brain activity. It is possible.

That said, it would be very worrying if this happened, and we are pretty certain in practice that the two things, brains and consciousness, always go together. The philosopher Descartes notoriously thought than animals had working brains without any feelings, and we can't prove he was wrong. We (most of us) just find it a very repulsive thought, and would refuse to cut a dog up while its brain was working. Plenty of people believe their dead dogs have gone to heaven, and presumably the dogs have not taken their physical brains with them. These dog-lovers might be wrong, they might be believing something that is very unlikely, but they are not believing the impossible.

I am afraid that if you want to know whether you can think without your brain, you will just have to wait and see. If you cannot think without your brain, you will never find out. In the meanwhile, I don't advise making any experiments to find out. However, we do have the disciples claiming that they saw a dead person. That is not a *proof*, because they might have been deluded, or perhaps there never were such experiences, and later on people decided that there must have been. I myself think it is pretty unlikely that they were either deluded or deceitful, but there you are.

But maybe Jesus had a brain. He just got up, walked out of the tomb . . . and then what? If it was an ordinary human brain, it must have taken up some space, and it must have been located inside an ordinary human head. Ordinary human heads do not appear suddenly out of nowhere (John 20:26), walk through locked doors (John 20:19), instantly change so much that people no longer recognize them (Luke 24:16), or vanish just as quickly as they appeared (Luke 24:31). But the accounts in the New Testament say that this is just what Jesus did. Where was Jesus when he was not appearing to the disciples? Did he have a secret hide-out somewhere in Jerusalem? And then, when he "ascended into heaven," did he really start rising into the air until he reached escape-velocity and shot through the clouds towards outer space? How could he breathe in outer space, and where was he going? To the moon? To another galaxy? Perhaps, if he cannot go faster than light, he is still going, far away in the depths of intergalactic space.

Once you face up to such questions, it becomes clear that the Jesus who appeared to the disciples did not do so in an *ordinary* human body. It was indeed an "appearance," a pretty solid one by all accounts, something like an avatar in a virtual-reality game. According to at least one New Testament account (1 Peter 3:19), after his death Jesus visited, and preached to people in *Sheol*, the world of the dead, and according to more accounts he appeared for shortish periods to the disciples, before leaving this world for ever.

Where was his brain, his ordinary physical human brain? I think an appropriate term would be that it was "assumed into heaven." It ceased to exist as a physical brain in our spacetime. It was changed into another form, which was not in this spacetime at all. We could not get into that other spacetime by moving in any direction from here. It is a different space, a different sort of space.

This might seem odd, but it is not in fact very odd to physicists, who talk quite glibly about "alternative universes" and spaces. What we are talking about when we talk about resurrection is another set of spatial dimensions, where the laws are quite different. In that space, Jesus might have a brain, but it would not be an ordinary physical brain, so he would have a consciousness that did not depend upon an ordinary physical brain. That causal link would have been cut. We have seen that the causal link between one brain and its consciousness *could* be cut. Now, with the birth of Christianity, we have a claim, based on experience, that it *has* been cut.

What was unusual about the resurrection was not that somebody survived death. To millions of people, that possibility has always seemed obvious. It was that a dead person could appear in this space in a visible and tangible way—and even that is not as odd as all that. There are quite a few records of dead people appearing. The special thing about Jesus' appearances is that they were taken to confirm his status as the divinely anointed spiritual King of Israel.

The resurrection of Jesus was certainly extraordinary. His body disappeared, and he appeared to some disciples "in another form" (Mark 16:12). But it is not as extraordinary as all that, since it is within the bounds of logical possibility, and if you think there is a Supreme Spirit that wishes to manifest the fact that human lives can be fulfilled after the death of their physical bodies, this seems like a good way to do it.

## WAS JESUS REAL?

Even the resurrection of Jesus, however, just sounds like a historical fact, an event that happened long ago. What has it got to do with today? That is where the singing and hand-waving in that little room in Jerusalem come into the picture. Because what the disciples then experienced was that they were suddenly "filled with the Holy Spirit" (Acts 2:1–4).

Just as Jesus, during his life, had forgiven sins, and blessed his followers with a spirit of joy and peace, so now the Spirit of Jesus was felt in the innermost lives of the disciples, bringing the divine wisdom and love, forgiveness and friendship, into their lives. The Spirit was even sometimes described as "the risen Christ within," a new and continuing presence and power within the hearts of men and women, that emanated from the resurrected Lord.

That is what distinguishes Christian faith from myth. It has a historical point of origin. It is rooted in the experience of the disciples, an experience of being filled with the power of the Spirit, causing them to turn from a depressed remnant into an energizing force. Their message was that the crucified Jesus had, by his resurrection, been declared the spiritual King of Israel, that through him sins could be forgiven, and that he would in the last days come in his kingdom with glory.

From this rather small event on the fringes of the Roman Empire, grew up a worldwide spiritual movement that proclaimed divine judgment, forgiveness, and a new life and relationship to God, produced by the inner power of the Spirit. This is the heart of Christian faith. It has its origin in the long development of monotheism within Judaism, and in the traumatic moment of spiritual renewal that followed the belief that Jesus, who had been crucified as a criminal and royal pretender, had been raised to live with God. As such, he became the channel of the life-giving power of the divine Spirit to the hearts of men and women.

It is quite natural that mythic elements, which tend to belong to all sacred narratives, should accumulate around the figure of Jesus. But what came to be the Gospels, compiled from memories of the historical Jesus and new experiences of the risen Christ in the early communities of disciples, preserve the earliest witnesses to the life and teachings of Jesus, as they were perceived by his disciples. It is the continuing presence of the Spirit, which they experienced, that gives spiritual power to people in every generation.

I suppose many people would think this is a down-grading of the Bible. In a sense, they are right. It is a denial that there is a magic infallible book that tells us all we need to know about the spiritual life. But the earliest disciples did not have such a book. What they had were texts they considered inspired scriptures (which became incorporated into what Christian call the Old Testament), but they felt that these texts could only be rightly understood in dialogue with the story of Jesus and their ongoing experience of the Holy Spirit. The texts were not self-sufficient guides to the life of faith and so they were not infallible.

As any Jew will tell you, Jesus' disciples had to be very selective about their searches of Scripture. Was Jesus going to be a handsome and altogether desirable beloved (Song of Solomon 5:10–16)? Or was he to be quite ugly, with "nothing in his appearance that we should desire him" (Isaiah 53:2)? Was he going to be someone who "shall break [the nations] with a rod of iron, and dash them in pieces like a potter's vessel" (Psalm 2:9)? Or was he going to be a kindly shepherd, leading a little flock of sheepish people into pleasant pastures (Psalm 23:1–2)? All these things are in the Old Testament, so if you are going to take them as prophecies of Jesus, you have to be pretty selective.

It wasn't even very clear what Jesus' relation to the Torah, the biblical Law, was. Did he think it should all be kept to the smallest detail (Matthew 5:17)? Or did he ignore it when he felt like it (Mark 7:19)?

There was some reason in the Jewish tradition to think there would one day be a Messiah. But the Old Testament is very unspecific about what the Messiah would be. Some have thought the Messiah would be a politician. Some have thought the Messiah might stand for a committee or a political party. Some thought it might be Elijah, come back to life. I do not suppose any of them thought the Messiah would die as a criminal, after criticizing the religious authorities of Israel. And I do not think any of them thought the Messiah would be divine. I did once ask an eminent Rabbi what the Messiah would be, and he said, "God knows." So that is about it.

Given what they knew and believed about Jesus, the first disciples could look back at the Old Testament Scriptures and pick out the bits that seemed to point to Jesus. They possibly even imagined some stories about Jesus' life by making them fulfillments of bits of the Old Testament. Jesus walking on the water is a possible example. Jesus might have walked on water. But why should he bother, when he could have hired a boat? Where was he going? And if he could do that, why did he ever ride in a boat anyway, as he apparently did? It would usually have been cheaper and healthier to walk.

One explanation is that this "event" was put in because in Psalm 77:19 the Lord God is said to walk on the waves of the sea. Saying that Jesus walked on the waves of Galilee would be a good way of "fulfilling" that prophecy, and showing that he was the Lord. Here is a mythic element, derived from a metaphor in the Old Testament describing God as dominating the sea, representing the waters of chaos, now used to express Jesus' divine authority.

The fact probably is that belief in Jesus' divine authority came first, quickly followed by "finding" a prophecy about water-walking in the Bible, and then completed by having Jesus conveniently fulfil the prophecy. That is certainly one foolproof way of finding prophecies about Jesus in the Old Testament. But it is a little bit suspect as a proof that Jesus was the Messiah.

Belief that Jesus was chosen by God to be the expression and channel of the divine Spirit does not depend on him walking on the sea. As a matter of fact, I think it rather trivializes and degrades the whole idea of spiritual authority. Is it really a good thing for someone to say, "I am a supreme spiritual teacher. To prove it I will just take a stroll on the sea without getting wet. That should really impress you"? I myself would certainly be impressed. But I would be impressed by his skills at magic, not by his spiritual authority. And I would think, "If you have to do that sort of thing to prove you are spiritually wise, you have a very odd idea of what spiritual wisdom is." And I wouldn't trust you an inch.

The world is full of spiritual fakes, and I know at least one person (a woman, as it happens) who thinks she is Jesus, and two or three who think they are Napoleon—strange how they tend to think they are somebody famous. One of my favorites was Krishnamurti, the late nineteenth-century Indian philosopher and mystic. Annie Besant, one of the founders of Theosophy, proclaimed when he was young that he was going to be the coming world saviour. But when he reached maturity, Krishnamurti said, "No I'm not." So, he was not a spiritual fake, but she does at least seem to have been mistaken.

This is getting rather worrying again. If there are so many fakes in the world, might not Jesus have been one of them, or might his disciples, if they could invent such amazing miracles, really have been con-men? Plenty of people have suggested this. I have seen what many, including many members of the minority Muslim group the Ahmadiyya, believe to be the grave of Jesus in Kashmir, where he is supposed to have gone after having recovered from his injuries in a failed crucifixion attempt. Some authors have made lots of money by claiming that Jesus married Mary Magdalene and went to France, and had a lot of children, who feature in various novels. Other novelists "know" that Mary was hidden away by the disciples, who made up lots of stuff about her son Jesus in order to become famous, but she knew that he was "just a naughty little boy," in the words of the Monty Python sketch.

Some of these stories are so odd that they can make you despair of human nature, and think that everyone is either a knave or a fool. There are certainly lots of knaves and fools around. But isn't it a slight exaggeration to think that everyone is like that? For a start, I know that *I* am not. You might think I am, admittedly, but that is not my fault. On the whole, I think that some people, really quite a lot of people, are morally upright, intelligent, and trustworthy. You just have to be careful.

There are some tests of knavery and stupidity, after all. You can try to see whether a person is morally sincere and thoughtful, has wide knowledge, sympathetic understanding, capacity to reason validly, and practical experience. Sometimes, we can be pretty sure that a person is morally heroic, giving their lives for the sake of others, for example. We can be pretty sure when a person has more insight, experience, or understanding than we have.

There are morally wise, compassionate, intelligent and wise people. They are rather rare, and we can sometimes be mistaken about who they are. If we are lucky enough to meet them (I have met a few) we are right to respect and admire them. Looking at the reports of Jesus' life and teaching, even if we admit they are often mythically enhanced, it seems to me as though he was indeed a heroically good and wise man with a profound insight into the divine nature and purpose, not a fool or a knave or someone who was chronically deluded.

There is a bit of faith in this judgment, of course. We cannot be sure, we cannot prove, that he was good and wise and knowledgeable about things of the spirit. But we have enough to make a positive judgment reasonable. And here is the crucial point about faith: we might have a present experience of a spiritual presence that helps us to be better and wiser, and that is life-enhancing and joyful. If we can connect this present experience with the historical person of Jesus, then our faith will not just be about someone who died a long time ago. It will be about a person who once walked the roads of ancient Galilee and Judea, and who still lives in a different spiritual form that continues to be a channel of divine love and wisdom.

If I am really pushed, I will have to admit that I cannot be *certain* that the historical Jesus really was as depicted in the Gospels, or that after his death he really was glorified as the Saviour of the world and Lord of the kingdom of God. If I got to heaven and found out that Jesus had been a mistaken prophet of the end of history, and that he is not now, in however metaphorical a sense, "sitting at the right hand of God," I would have to admit that I had been wrong. I must emphasize that I do *not* think I am wrong. But just suppose I was. Then I would still say that I was right about the most important thing, which is that the image of Jesus presented in the Gospels depicts what a person who is truly the authentic manifestation and mediator of God would be like. The Spirit I experience and describe as the power of Christ within me would still be what I take to be an authentic experience of a God of self-giving love. I can truly worship God in and through that image of Christ. Even if it was historically inaccurate, it is spiritually authentic.

Of course, if you push me even further, I would have to admit that I cannot even be logically certain that God exists. But in that case, I would presumably never get to heaven, since it would not exist, so I would never have to admit my mistake. The point is that I can reasonably be totally committed to belief in God, in the biblically presented image of Christ as the authentic revelation of God, and in Jesus as a historical figure who is reliably, if not inerrantly, depicted in that biblical image. I cannot be *logically certain* of any of these things. But I can *reasonably believe* that they are true. If the disciples of Jesus had not believed in and reflected on their experiences of the Spirit of Jesus, a Jesus whom they had known during his earthly life, the ideas of God as self-giving love and of the human hope for eternal life in God would probably never have existed. The fact that these ideas do exist and transform the spiritual lives of believers to this day, is good evidence that the Gospels, which embody many memories of Jesus by those who had known him personally, give a pretty accurate portrait of the historical Jesus. It is true, however, that we cannot believe this on purely historical grounds. We can believe it largely because of the continuing transforming power of the present spiritual experience of Christ.

The man many disciples had known as a wise and good spiritual guide, had, after his death, they believed, been raised up to God and had seemed to pour out upon them the Spirit of truth, wisdom, and love that they had seen in him. It is this continuing presence that Christians worship, revere, admire, and seek to shape their lives upon. If this presence is a power making for goodness, happiness, truth, love, and wisdom, then there is good reason for believing that Jesus expressed such a power in his earthly life.

## EXTRAORDINARY EVENTS

What about Jesus' reported miracles, then? Are they all mistaken attempts to enhance his spiritual authority? I have been skeptical, even cynical, about some of them. But actually my attitude might better be called agnostic, even reverently agnostic. Because I do believe in the reality of a spiritual dimension that underlies everything that we see and touch and sense. And I do believe that this dimension, because it is real, has effects in the material world that we experience from day to day. Minds can affect bodies; Spirit can affect matter. If a person like Jesus mediates the spiritual in a profound way, those effects are likely to be more pronounced and obvious.

What you think about miracles is going to depend on your more basic beliefs about what is real, about what sorts of things exist. If you think nothing but matter exists, and that matter always acts according to regular laws of nature, you are not going to think that miracles happen. Miracles are, by definition, extraordinary events with a spiritual significance. The material is altered in some way by some sort of mental, psychical, or spiritual, force. If you are open to that possibility, you are on your way to thinking that there might be miracles. They will probably be associated with people or places where there is an especially strong or focussed spiritual power.

The biggest miracle in Christianity is the resurrection. I have already suggested that was not an ordinary body coming back to life and walking around. Jesus was not a Zombie. It was the appearance of a *spiritual* body— a person in the spiritual realm—for fairly short periods and over a fairly short stretch of time, to some disciples. If this was a genuine appearance, not a delusion, then here was matter being affected by a spiritual reality. If you think that there is a spiritual realm that can affect the material, and if you think that people whose bodies die and decay can continue to exist in a spiritual realm, the resurrection will not be quite such an odd event.

Taking this a bit further, if Jesus always was a uniquely strong channel of spiritual power, we might suspect that this power would show itself in some extraordinary ways. We would be surprised if Jesus performed no miracles. Most of his reported miracles were healing miracles. If you think faith healing could be genuine, you might expect that Jesus would be a faith healer, a person who was able to heal many types of mental and physical illness. His spiritual power could also be shown in his insight into the minds of others, and in his ability to address their deepest needs and aspirations.

If that is true, why don't I simply accept the biblical accounts of his healing miracles and his ability to know what others were thinking at face value? There are three main reasons. First, I think many accounts of miracles in the Bible are grossly exaggerated—or, to put it more kindly, mythically enhanced. You can see this in the different accounts of the crossing of the Red Sea (the "sea of reeds," actually). According to many biblical scholars, the final account, with the sea standing up like a wall, and then crashing down on the Pharaoh and all his army, is a very much heightened account from some earlier versions. Some scholars point out that Egyptian records do not mention any such event, and that the Pharaoh was most unlikely to have been personally involved. Some even suggest that only a few dozen slaves were involved, and that they picked their way through some marshes near the mouth of the Nile, where a small Egyptian pursuing force got bogged down. So, the exodus consisted of two dozen slaves wading through a bog. Not quite a Hollywood version of events!

Whatever exactly happened, it seems that some exaggeration has crept in. Any responsible reading of the biblical text should make it clear that scholars interpret it in very different ways, and that the spiritual message is that God wills the freeing of slaves from oppression. Such liberation is one of the founding events of the nation of Israel, however it happened. You can believe that, without believing that things were quite as extraordinary as the text says.

This leads on to the second main reason for being rather agnostic about biblical records of miracles. The Gospels report that Jesus exorcised many demons, who tended to call out "You are the Son of God" as they were ejected from people, in one notable case, into a herd of pigs, which then jumped over a cliff into the sea. Modern medical science has no knowledge of demons, and though mental illnesses of many kinds are common, such illnesses are largely put down to malfunctions of the brain, and treated with drugs. At the time of Jesus, people did believe in demons causing illnesses, but we prefer to believe in viruses, which do not shout, "You are the Son of God," as they are attacked with antiviral drugs.

Moreover, Jesus is reported as healing hundreds of people instantaneously (though one or two at a time, admittedly), even at a distance, and that seems rather excessive. If he could do that, why did he not just heal everybody in the world and have done with it? If he was omnipotent, he could easily have done that. But if his powers were that of an especially effective faith healer, his healings, while very impressive, would not have been quite so thoroughgoing.

This in turn leads onto a third reason for agnosticism about biblical miracle reports: nothing like them exists in the world today. Perhaps demons have gone into hiding. Or perhaps nobody has enough faith. Perhaps Jesus was quite unique in his powers—but remember he said that his disciples would do even greater works than his. So, we would expect a great many more miracles than we get.

There are many claims to miracles. There are snake-handling Baptists, mostly in Arkansas, who, believing Jesus' promise that snakes would not harm them, demonstrate their faith by caressing snakes. True, some of them have died from snakebites—lack of faith, I suppose. As far as I know, even in Arkansas there is not a sect of one-eyed Baptists, who take seriously Jesus' command to pull your right eye out if you find it offensive. Perhaps their right eyes are never offensive, and they are all two-eyed completely inoffensive Baptists—good on them.

All in all, I think it is reasonable to say that things that happened two thousand years ago were not entirely dissimilar from things that happen today. If so, while I am prepared to believe in faith-healing and in some forms of telepathy, I remain agnostic about claims that two thousand years ago in the Middle East there were evil demons who complained loudly and bitterly as they were inserted into herds of pigs. Anyway, I feel sorry for the pigs, who had done nothing to deserve their watery and demon-filled fate.

Well, as I say, I am agnostic. I have reasons for not taking some of the biblical accounts of miracles as sober literal truths. I do admit that they could have happened just as recorded, but Jesus did say that he would not perform any miracles to prove that he had divine authority (Matthew 12:39). I rather think that if someone possessed supreme divine authority, he (or she) would not show it by creating food or diamond rings or even Cadillac autos out of thin air (though that would certainly be impressive).

On the one hand, Jesus' reported miracles are too small to be believable—he could have fed the whole population of Israel, not just five or six thousand of them. On the other hand, his miracles are too great—they exceed all known bounds of human psychic powers. I incline to think that Jesus performed miracles, but only medium-sized ones. But then that is perhaps because I am an Anglican, and we like to see evidence of a little spiritual power, but nothing too extreme or enthusiastic.

## MOZART AND THE PROPHETS

Even on such a reduced view of Jesus' extraordinary powers, there remain some big claims about his uniqueness as a human being. According to John's Gospel (and it is interesting that statements like this only occur in this Gospel), Jesus said, "I am the Way, the Truth, and the Life" (John 14:6). This has led many Christians to say that unless a person believes in Jesus, they cannot be on a path towards salvation. Probably all my first Christian friends thought that. But is this really so, or is this another fossil of fundamentalism?

John (whoever exactly John was) has a habit of putting his beliefs about the risen Jesus into the mouth of the historical person Jesus. John believes Jesus to be the incarnation of the eternal Wisdom and Word of God. It is this divine Wisdom that is the way to God, the deepest truth of reality, and the principle of true life. It is not Jesus qua human being who is the way to God. It is Jesus *as the mediator of the divine Wisdom*. If Jesus was truly the embodiment of this Wisdom, he would have had a uniquely intense and intimate experience and love of God. He would have been in a better position to know God and the way to God than the vast majority of people.

If this seems unrealistic, the example of music might help a little. Just as Mozart really was a better composer than most other people, so true prophets are in a better position to know what God is like than most people. They may still not be infallible, but they are spiritual leaders.

The trouble is, spiritual leaders still disagree, it seems. Mohammed, Gautama, and Jesus often say different things. They are, by general agreement, people of great spiritual knowledge, ability, and insight.

We cannot compare Mozart with Wagner, to say who was best. They belong in different traditions. They are both geniuses, but write music in different styles, using instruments in different ways, and having different ideals. Can we say that about Mohammed and Jesus? I think that we not only can, but we must, to account for the differences between them. They are spiritual masters, who perfect a specific religious tradition, and also transform that tradition in new and unique ways.

Jesus transforms the idea of a Messiah, or liberating King of Israel, into that of a universal liberator from evil. Mohammed transforms the idea of the commanding God of Abraham and Isaac into a God of universal mercy and compassion. Gautama transforms the idea of the world-renouncer into that of a conqueror of the egoistic self. They each generate a new model of a spiritual path, arising from but transforming existing models. They are heroes of the Spirit.

There are many paths of spiritual self-transformation. But they all tend to assert that they alone have the full truth about spiritual reality. The time has come to look for a more convergent view, and say that there are many differing aspects or perspectives on spiritual reality. They might not all be equally adequate. Nor will it be obvious that one is better in all respects than the others. We can adopt one, (or more probably find ourselves tending to think in terms of one more than others, because of our education and culture). We are almost bound to think that our view is the most adequate one we can find. Christians are bound to think that in Jesus we find the most adequate revelation of God, and that there are good reasons for thinking that. But we are not bound to think that the Christian faith is perfect as it stands. We can go on to modify it if it seems necessary in the light of new scientifically based knowledge, new moral insights arising from changing social conditions, and greater understanding of other spiritual traditions. But we do not have to say that everyone else is wholly mistaken, and insist that we are wholly right.

## LOOKING FOR THE COSMIC CHRIST

Anglicans on the whole have a rather flexible view of what you need to believe to be a Christian. But it is pretty safe to say that they generally are prepared to think that Jesus was the Messiah (they usually prefer the Greek translation, "the Christ"). It is hard to escape that thought if you go to church. But what does it mean? For some of those who heard Jesus speak, it probably meant that he would in the near future liberate Israel from Roman domination, and make Israel great again. The trouble is, that never happened. And it is not obvious that was what Jesus was on about anyway. The Christian church soon got rid of the idea of Jewish political liberation, and replaced it with the idea that Christ was a cosmic figure who might liberate the whole world from sin.

This led to a new interpretation of Jesus, which is given in many New Testament letters, some of them by Paul, that the Messiah, the Christ, is the liberator, not from political enemies of Israel, but from anger, hatred, and inordinate self-love, and is the human embodiment of the eternal Wisdom or Word of God, who unites finite beings to the divine, so that in the end all things will be united "in Christ." You get this interpretation in the Gospel of John, and also in the letters to the Colossians and Ephesians, and it is probably a very early strand of teaching about Jesus.

Today we are able to expand this vision even further, now that we know the universe is so old and vast, with billions of galaxies, stars, and planets. Paul almost certainly believed, at least early in his life, that history would end quite soon with the return of Jesus in glory, so that Jesus would reign on the earth. Some of his letters are filled with the fantastic symbolism of the Old Testament prophets about a final catastrophic battle between good and evil (Armageddon), in which evil is finally destroyed and the Chosen One of God comes on the clouds to finally bring peace on earth. Some early Christians thought this would happen soon, even within their lifetimes (1 Thessalonians 4:17). I am not sure that I would like to find myself, as that text suggests, suddenly flying through the air and getting caught up in the clouds to meet the Lord and stay there forever. There are other places I would rather be, and I simply do not have a head for heights!

Actually, there is not much chance of that, since I would almost certainly be one of those "left behind" to face the music. Anyway, none of that happened, and it was quite a relief for me to find out that all that biblical symbolism functioned something like the Marvel comics of the ancient world, in which imaginary superheroes destroy various evil monsters who threaten the universe. The reality all that symbolism stands for is that there is a real battle between good and evil, which goes on every day in our earthly lives. There will be an ultimate triumph of good over evil, and Christians believe that Christ, in a scarcely imaginable form, will be disclosed to all as the eternal Wisdom of God and the pattern and purpose of history.

As such he will, as the Nicene Creed (I have not quite forgotten that I am talking about that from time to time) says, "come again with glory to judge both the quick [i.e., the living] and the dead." But there will be no actual bloody battle, no actual trumpets, and no actual man descending rapidly from the sky, no actual throne on which the man will sit, and no actual sheep and goats standing around waiting to be judged, either. Most importantly, the Christian faith is that "mercy triumphs over judgement" (James 2:13), and "we have our hope set on the living God, who is the saviour of all people" (1 Timothy 4:10). The final thought, then, is that though we should take seriously the idea that evil will fall under a just judgment, the hope of eventual union with God is a hope not for a few, but for "all people."

Anyway, now that we know we are only a tiny part of a vast universe, and that this planet will be swallowed up by the sun in about five billion years, we can accept that a human Jesus will not return to earth on a cloud. How will this affect our view of Jesus? We can say that Jesus embodied a truly cosmic Christ, who possibly expresses the divine in billions of finite forms in billions of finite places, and unites them all to the divine life. At the end of this spacetime, we will not see a human being seated on a seat next to God. We will see a billion finite forms expressing the divine in a billion ways, but always revealing a God of love who wishes to include all the good things of time in the divine life. That being is truly expressed for us on this planet in the person of Jesus, but we should never think that this is the *only* finite form that the infinite God can take.

Once we have got that far, it might occur to us that we do not have to travel to other galaxies to find people who have never heard of Jesus. There are plenty of people on earth who have not heard of Jesus, who have been brought up in very different religious traditions. What is true of beings in other galaxies is likely to be true of them too. God desires their salvation; salvation is only through the power of the Wisdom of God. So, doesn't it make sense to say that Christ is present to them too? The Wisdom of God can be expressed in the Qu'ran, in the teachings of the Buddha, in the Guru Granth, and in other forms too. If the eternal Word can take the form of a little green alien, surely it can take many forms that we can hardly imagine. These forms may not all be of equal adequacy, and they will be affected by the very different background beliefs of those who experience them, and not all these beliefs can be true. Yet surely Christ the eternal Word can be present in some way in many different religious traditions in the world.

I believe the time has come when Christians should openly embrace this wider vision of Christ. After all, it is found in a number of New Testament writings, like that of the letter to the Colossians, which says that "through him [Christ] God was pleased to reconcile to himself all things, whether on earth or in heaven" (Colossians 1, 20). When I was a fundamentalist, I somehow missed passages like that, or tried to argue that they didn't really mean "all things." Despite my many objections to biblical literalism, those were maybe passages I really should have taken more literally.

## AM I THE ONLY PERSON WHO IS RIGHT?

The vast majority of Anglicans regard the Scriptures as generally reliable accounts of Jesus and of the beliefs of quite early disciples. They accept what they regard as central to those beliefs as caused by divine revelation, even if such revelation is partly conditioned by the cultural and historical conditions of the age. They regard the early Christian councils as important developments of Christian belief that need to be taken into account in any modern statements of belief, though again they will be seen as culturally and historically conditioned and not totally free from error. And they regard Calvin and Aquinas, for instance, as important Christian theologians, whose views it is important to consider, though they should not be slavishly followed. No one should ever be given the sense that their own interpretation of faith, or that of their favorite preacher or writer, is the one and only truth, and that people who have other views are not "real" Christians.

For there are a number of different ideas about what the true faith is. Opus Dei Catholics would have a very different true faith than Strict and Particular Baptists, who may in turn split into the Even Stricter and More Particular Baptists, leaving behind the Fairly Flexible and Not Quite So Particular Baptists.

What can stop people thinking that they have got hold of an absolutely certain and infallible truth, when they know that lots of other people have got hold of quite different absolutely certain and infallible truths? Unfortunately, these sets of absolutely certain and infallible truths happen to contradict each other. This is definitely a problem.

Many Christians have a very strong belief that Christ is an authentic manifestation of God, and that this is the most adequate manifestation of which they know. This belief may be so strong that they can hardly understand how anyone could deny it. Yet they really know that only a minority of the world's population (albeit a very large minority) agree with them. So how can they be certain?

Surely nothing can be certainly true unless it can be demonstrated to the satisfaction of all intelligent and informed people. "Ah, but," they may each say, "it is not that I am more intelligent than any else. It is only that I, humble as I am, have been chosen by God to be the recipient of this special knowledge."

It is not particularly humble to think that one has been specially chosen by God. And when other people also think they have been chosen by God to think different things, this is bound to make you wonder if you might be exaggerating slightly. In fact, you should quickly realize that at least one of you must be mistaken. From which it follows that *believing* God has told you something does not guarantee that God has *really* done so, or even that there is really a God. And from that it follows that however certain you are that God has told you something, *you might be wrong.* And if you might be wrong, you cannot really be absolutely theoretically certain. QED.

It looks as though you might feel quite confident that something is true, even though you have to admit that you might be wrong. Does this make sense? I actually think it does. You might feel confident about a belief, you might even bet your life on it, even when it might be mistaken. For instance, if you are lost in the desert, you may have to start walking in one direction, staking your life on the belief, or the hope, that it is the right way, and you may actually have good reasons for feeling confident that your chosen direction is right, even though you could be making a mistake.

So, you can commit your life to the belief that Jesus is the Son of God, even when you accept the possibility that you might be mistaken. That is what faith is! It is a passionate commitment made in face of objective uncertainty. That commitment is, however, one that makes for good and for human fulfilment. It is one that seems to you to make the best sense of your knowledge and experience of the world. That is probably what most really basic human commitments are, in politics, morality, human relations, science, and religion. It is an unavoidable part of the human condition. It is not absolute theoretical certainty. But it is a deeply rational, and sometimes a personally compelling, venture of faith in goodness and understanding, of love of the good, and of hope for its fulfilment.

These thoughts have taken me quite a long way from fundamentalism, and its belief that there is only one narrow and exclusive way to God, which is available only to people who take the Bible, and especially the New Testament, literally. It is by reading the Bible that I have come to think that God desires the salvation of all, so that Jesus is the revelation of God's love for everyone, not of a few who have been selected by God for reasons we cannot understand. I retain, and am grateful for, the fundamentalist belief that Jesus lived and died and rose to glory to "take away the sin of the world." But once you begin to think about what "the world" is, you might tend to think that it includes more than a few Christians. Then you are on the way to believing that Christ is the saviour of all, whether they take the Bible literally or not. I have taken that way.

93

# CHAPTER SIX

## Coping with the Church

### HOW THE CHURCHES BEGAN (POSSIBLY)

As I GRADUALLY WORKED my way through all these knotty problems, I seemed to fit into the Anglican Church without too much trouble. I love church music, cathedral choirs, and dressing up, and I am quite fond of the odd whiff of incense. I like the fact that nobody asks me exactly what I believe, and that lots of different sorts of people seem to be there. But one question kept nagging me. Despite the fact that there might be many different religious traditions where the eternal Christ might be found, did Jesus found an organization, a church that all people were supposed to belong to in the end, and was it the Church of England? Some Anglicans might like to think so, but when Jesus was around, he probably did not know there was any such place as England (there wasn't, really), so I have to admit that sounds a bit unrealistic. Well, then, did Jesus found any church, and if so, which one? Jesus certainly did not set up an organization with a written constitution for which he wrote a creed, or set of orthodox beliefs. There is no record that he created a pope and a college of cardinals, much less an Archbishop of Canterbury or a Presiding Bishop of the Episcopal Church.

He did have disciples, and an inner group of twelve who were particularly important. When one of the twelve died, they appointed another (chosen by lot, not by Peter) to take his place. They required that person to be a witness to the resurrection, and someone who had known Jesus personally. So, there was an important group of twelve apostles. There is a suggestion that there was one apostle for each tribe of Israel, and that they would head the twelve tribes after the coming of the kingdom of God (Matthew 19:28).

The first disciples thought this might happen at any time, so there was not much need to think about the apostles having any successors, and there is no record of any plans about how that would be done.

Then Paul came along. He regarded himself as an apostle, on the slightly shaky ground that he had seen Jesus in a vision. He founded groups of believers all over the place, and he seemed to operate largely independently of the twelve in Jerusalem. In any case, most of the twelve soon disappear from the biblical records, except for one called James, who popped up briefly only to get beheaded (Acts 12:2). There is no strong evidence about what happened to them, though many traditions soon grew up. Paul thought that the leaders of the church in Jerusalem were probably Peter, James (a different James, described as the brother of Jesus), and John, but Paul added that he did not care much about who the leaders were (Galatians 2:6). There does not seem to have been a very centralised organization.

Paul's relation to the Jerusalem Christians is rather mysterious. He wrote (in a letter to the Galatians, which most scholars think really is by him) that he did not visit Jerusalem for three years after his spectacular conversion, and then he visited Peter for two weeks, and briefly met James, but no one else. He did not return to Jerusalem for fourteen years. The book of Acts, however, seems to have him in Jerusalem very early on, talking to the apostles. The Bible is clearly not a very clear witness on that.

We do know that James became the head of the Jerusalem church, while Peter escaped from prison and then disappears from the records. In the Book of Acts, chapter 12, verse 18, it says simply, "He [Peter] left, and went to another place." Of course, some people think he went to Rome, where he became the first pope. That may be true, but again there is unfortunately no evidence for it. Luke, who wrote Acts, does not seem to be very interested in where he went.

The most obvious thing about the early churches is that they were from the first an argumentative lot. One of the biggest arguments was about whether gentile converts should be circumcised (a rather painful business for adult men before anaesthetics came along). The main group at first was naturally enough in Jerusalem, and we know that James the brother of Jesus was a keen supporter of circumcision for everyone. He seems to have been persuaded by Peter and Paul, who found it hard to persuade gentiles to have important pieces of themselves cut off with a piece of flint, that this was not a good idea, but the Jerusalem Christians continued to attend the temple and keep the Jewish religious laws. There might well have been two main churches, one for Jews and one for gentiles. But the Jerusalem church, the Jewish one, disappeared from history when Jerusalem itself was destroyed by the Romans in 135 AD. Interestingly, a possible remnant of that church, the Ebionites, apparently denied the virgin birth. Since the brother of Jesus is supposed to have been part of that group, I suppose he would know. But little is certain on these matters.

Anyway, there were lots of local communities of disciples, many of them founded by Paul, and in the end the surviving ones became completely gentile. Were they founded by Jesus? They were certainly founded by people who were disciples of Jesus—quite a number of different people, most of whom are not remembered. It does not seem that there was just one institution with one leader, "the true church." There were many groups of Jesus-followers, and many of them had little connection with the original twelve. They had some things in common. They had no New Testament, they stressed "baptism in the Spirit," and kept up a communal meal in remembrance of Jesus. They worshipped the risen Christ, and believed themselves to be born again and "united in Christ." They were not united with one another, however, and the story of the developing church is a story of seemingly endless arguments and disagreements.

The leaders of local churches called themselves bishops (overseers). It was quite good being an elder, but it soon began to sound much better to be a bishop. Knowing human nature, one could predict that there would soon be archbishops too, as that sounds even better. I once met a charming and vivacious Pentecostalist pastor who was an archbishop. When I expressed surprise that such a young man could have such an exalted title, he said, "I used to be a bishop. But then I didn't get invited to international conferences. So I made myself an archbishop, and now I get invited to conferences all over the world." I have to say that "pope" sounds even better than archbishop, so it was always pretty predictable that one day somebody would call themselves a pope. In fact, there are in the world today a number of popes, but, as each of them would say, there is only one "real" pope. Guess which one that is?

Another high-status word is "patriarch," really meaning "Big Chief," and there were, and still are, a number of patriarchs, especially in the Eastern churches. Like royalty, they are to be addressed by such flattering phrases as "Your Eminence" or "Your Holiness." The form of address I like best is that of the Patriarch of the Romanian Orthodox Church. I met him once and, not knowing quite how to address him, I said, "Good morning, your Eminence." He drew himself up to his full and impressive stature, and said, "I am not an eminence. I am a beatitude." I would not be surprised if somewhere there is a church leader who is to be addressed as "Your remarkably holy and supremely admirable very high-upness." It does seem quite a long way from the Jesus who said that spiritual leaders should be those who serve and do not claim exalted privileges. But that is what happens when human beings get in control of religions.

After the destruction of the Jerusalem church, most of these early churches were in what is now Egypt, Syria, and Turkey. The cities of Alexandria, Antioch, and Constantinople became important centres of Christian thought. There was a little European outpost in Rome, which was after all the capital of the old Roman Empire, but it did not amount to much. However, things were about to change. The Roman Empire was falling apart, and Christians in Rome were at first a small and sometimes persecuted minority. But they claimed that both Peter and Paul had died in Rome (maybe they did), so the church was apostolic from two lines of descent.

Humans like to trace their ancestry, and they like to think that they are descended from somebody important. They also tend to think that the older something is the better. If a religious body can trace its teaching back to the Great Pyramids that is thought to be a wonderful thing. I suppose that according to that way of thought, if the Anglican Church could trace its teachings back to the Stone Age, that would be even more wonderful. Sometimes I am tempted to think that it can, and that it has never really left the Stone Age.

It is not much fun if you spend a lot of time and money tracing your ancestry, and records end up with somebody like Jimmy the odd job man in some remote Sumerian village. Much more satisfying to find that you are descended from Napoleon. If the Anglican Church could only trace its ancestry back to Henry VIII of England, that would be disappointing (even though one pope did award Henry the title of "Defender of the Faith"— rather prematurely, as it turned out). Fortunately, the Anglican Church can trace its ancestry back at least to some of the first disciples of Jesus, though it has certainly changed a lot since then.

But *all* churches have changed a lot since then. In fact, churches are changing all the time. When Roman Catholics feel like being very traditional, they usually go back to the Council of Trent, in 1545. They want the modern church to look very like that, even though very few people would dream of burning Protestants at the stake and riding around on horseback.

When Anglicans appeal to tradition, they usually only go back thirty years or so, when most of their old traditions were invented. In fact, people who want to go back in time always fail to do so, because they are being consciously conservative, whereas the people they would like to imitate were being consciously innovative at the time. There could hardly be a bigger difference than that.

Most churches do not really want to go back as far as the time of Jesus, when churches mostly consisted of little groups of people who met in houses, shared their goods in common, prophesied at boring length, and waved their hands in the air a lot. Today such things would be called cults, and most churches definitely think they are not cults.


## THE TRUE CHURCH, OR PERHAPS NOT

Sometimes we hear calls from groups of grumpy old Christians that we should return to the "old-time religion." They usually have no idea of what the old-time religion was, so what they do is start a new church of their own, and claim that *it* is the old-time religion. What they have not noticed is that Christianity went through at least two major revolutions in the first few centuries of its existence, and that we have no precise idea of what it was like before that. The very first disciples of Jesus had no New Testament to tell them what to believe, they had no body of "orthodox" doctrines. They were all Jewish, and, until Paul came along, probably all kept the Jewish festivals, food laws, and customs. Many of them probably thought Jesus would return in a few years, gather all the scattered Jewish tribes from the far corners of the earth back to Jerusalem, where they would keep the Torah (the Jewish law) scrupulously, and make the Jerusalem temple, with its old sacrifices of animals restored, the center of worship for the whole world. The twelve apostles would rule the twelve tribes of Israel, and the world would accept the universal sovereignty of Israel. Gentiles were outsiders, and if they wanted to follow Jesus, they had to covert to Judaism first.

This Jewish group centred on the Jerusalem temple and its worship and keeping the Torah in its smallest details is almost certainly not what grumpy old Christians have in mind. But it probably is the nearest thing to the genuinely old-time religion. Therefore, those who want the really old-time religion ought to throw out the New Testament, stop eating pork sausages, and get circumcised at once.

COPING WITH THE CHURCH

Well, perhaps they prefer the sort of Christianity that existed after the first revolution, when Peter and Paul and James persuaded the disciples to invite gentiles to full membership of their community, and accepted that gentile Christians did not need to be circumcised. In fact, some new churches that claim to be returning to the old religion are often more like this early gentilized church. They often speak in tongues, wave their hands in the air, meet in rooms in their houses, and have informal associations with carefully selected like-minded groups of followers of Jesus. But if they were really old-time, they would have no creeds and would not yet have agreed whether Jesus and especially the Holy Spirit were truly divine, and if so in what sense. They would be pretty flexible about their beliefs, and would not dream of consulting books about theology (which would not even exist). They would have public sessions where they all confessed their sins (very embarrassing), and they would share their goods in common (very irritating). They would obey the state authorities, whatever they were, except that they would not agree to fight in wars or worship Emperors or go to law to get what they wanted. They would set themselves apart from society, and vow not to own or pursue large cars and houses, or fame and money.

I have a sneaking admiration for such people, though I could not now be one of them. Dr. Johnson, who represents quite well the attitudes of many Anglicans, said, "Enthusiasm is a very horrid thing." Those who attend Anglican churches regularly know that we have taken his advice to heart. Enthusiastic hand-waving is all rather too extreme for most Anglicans.

Anyway, Christian faith went through a second revolution in the first two or three centuries. It became an imperial religion, divided into two main parts, as the Roman Empire was—Eastern (Byzantine) and Western (Catholic), with lots of smaller groups, most of them imitating imperial rites and customs as well as they could.

The imperial tradition began when the Emperor Constantine became a Christian in AD 312, and Christianity not long afterwards became the official religion of the Roman Empire. Once Christianity became fashionable, it began to suffer the fate of all fashions. It became beloved by the rich and famous, and a quick route to influence and power for the leaders of the new imperial church. At this time there were a number of patriarchs (that is even better than being an archbishop), with Rome having a primacy of honour, but the other patriarchs—like those of Antioch, Alexandria, and, slightly later, Constantinople and Jerusalem—did not think they were subjected to

99

the authority of Rome. However, Rome did not agree with them, and went to great lengths to assert that it did have authority over everybody else. When one of the last Roman Emperors handed over his imperial title of Supreme Pontiff to the Bishop of Rome, the Romans completed their successful claim to be the one universal church. That bid was never completely successful, and there remained many churches (like the Eastern churches— e.g., Greek, Syrian, Coptic, and Nestorian) that regarded the Roman pope as something of an upstart. But in the course of history, many of those Eastern churches were swamped by Islam or had to be content with being minority faiths in India and China, while the Roman church—now calling itself the "catholic" or universal church—became more and more politically active and powerful in Western Europe and later in most European colonies.

When they became imperial, most churches became very hierarchical in nature, with the top people (bishops and above) making all the decisions, while all the rest were confined to reciting devoutly, "We are but silly sheep." Women were excluded from all positions of authority; they were much too informal, friendly, and sensible for membership of the priests' club, though the priests showed their great appreciation of women by themselves wearing gorgeous robes, and they also honoured women by allowing them to make tea and sandwiches.

The main activity of the new imperial church was to sponsor furious arguments about topics that nobody could understand. There were arguments about whether Jesus was created or begotten, or had just emerged from the Father by accident. And there were arguments about whether God was one substance or two or three substances, whether Jesus was two persons or just one, whether substances were the same as persons, how many beings there were in a Being, and whether it was better to sit on top of a pillar for twenty years or to get a decent job.

Since there was no way of getting a definitive answer to these arguments, the bishops took to hitting each other and declaring each other heretical (heresy was declared to be a bad thing). Then the Byzantine Emperor would step in and tell them which view was orthodox (i.e., the one he preferred) and which views were heretical. Different Emperors turned out to have different opinions on these matters, so various bishops kept getting exiled, sacked, then called back again when the Emperor's mood changed.

The bishops had the good idea of burning all books and speeches by the people they disagreed with, and they were then able to say that all the bishops agreed with each other. They even persuaded the Holy Spirit to agree with them (or so they said). They felt free to eliminate everyone who disagreed, so while there had perhaps once been some other disagreeable bishops, they were soon mysteriously not around anymore.

Is this the old-time religion? I am not sure. It seems that when people long for the good old days, they are all dreaming of quite different things. Perhaps the only factor that holds all these dreams together is that none of the churches they are dreaming about really existed.

Some people are dreaming about the golden age of the Catholic Church, when heretics could be burned at the stake, literature could be censored by church authorities, all non-Catholics could be sent to hell, and salvation could be obtained by the payment of a small sum of money or by walking around a church in Rome seven times.

Other people, however, dream about the golden age of the Protestant Reformation, when Catholics could be burned at the stake, people could be fined for not going to church, all Catholics, Jews, and Muslims could be sent to hell, especially the pope, and salvation could be obtained by saying "I love Jesus" in a loud voice.

Probably we will have to be content with churches as they actually are. The most obvious thing about them is that they are all very different. Pope Benedict XVI said that there was only one church, which happened to be the one he belonged to. All the rest were not churches at all, but only "ecclesial communities." Most people had always thought that churches were ecclesial communities, so it is hard to see what he was getting at. It is rather like saying that England is the only true country in the world, and all the rest are just sociopolitical communities. I think Pope Benedict meant that only those who accepted the pope (i.e., him) as their leader were really in the church. That would almost certainly exclude all the first generation of Christians, so the true church must have started a few centuries after Jesus' death, and even then, arguments continued for more centuries over whether the pope really was the leader of all Christians, and what sort of leader he was. It may well seem that in fact the Emperor Constantine was the real founder of the imperial church. It is certainly true that Constantine convened and controlled the great church councils and he was the one who began to turn the church into an imperial institution.

I guess it is true that all present Christian churches started sometime after the death of Jesus, and that they have all changed considerably over time. But churches, even some quite new ones, love to say that they were really founded by Jesus, and can be traced back to him by a mysterious process called the "apostolic succession." This requires that every true bishop has to have been blessed by another true bishop, and that this line of bishops goes right back to Jesus without a break.

There are some qualifications to this process. Every bishop is supposed to believe basically the same things as every other bishop. Since bishops used to spend most of their time claiming that other bishops were heretical, this seems a tough call. And since nobody knows exactly what the very first bishops believed, it seems to put a stop to any new developments of doctrine or even of thinking. I have myself been invited to be "properly" ordained by a properly blessed couple of rather suspect Eastern Orthodox bishops, for a fee of $500. This would make me a "proper priest," instead of the fake priest that I presumably am, according to them. Indeed, it is a fact that some properly blessed Roman Catholic bishops in France have ordained some women as priests. The official line, however, is that this does not make them priests. Presumably for the ceremony to work you have to have testicles (though you must agree not to use them, of course).

There is also a major problem about Paul and his friends. Paul was keen to insist that he did not owe his apostolate to any human person. He was certainly not appointed by the historical Jesus, and not by Peter either. So, he is a precedent for people setting themselves up as bishops because of their remarkable spiritual experiences. But perhaps we do not these days want people just to set themselves up as bishops because of some strange experience they have had, and proceed publicly to proclaim whatever comes into their heads.

On second thoughts, why not? If anyone can get people to read the Bible in their front room, to eat and drink in memory of Jesus, to pray together, and to feel the power of the divine Spirit within and among them, they have got a church. Indeed, that is the nearest thing to the truly old-time religion that probably existed about a century after the death of Jesus.

King Henry VIII is often said by non-Anglicans to have founded the Church of England, which later gave rise to the worldwide Anglican Communion. He certainly did not intend to do that. He intended to keep the Catholic faith as it then existed in place, except for accepting the authority of the pope, whom he did not like. This would have been a church very like the Eastern Orthodox churches, who did not like the pope either. Then things got complicated as Protestant Reformers got in on the act, and Puritans and Calvinists got key positions in the national church. The Church in

England became a mix of Catholic and Protestant, to which was later added a group of churches run by the idiot sons of the aristocracy who could not find a decent job. When other Anglican churches were started in other countries, they inherited this diversity. Consequently, the Anglican Communion is a very diverse set of churches, its main virtue being that it suited the sort of human beings who could not agree about anything. That may seem worrying to some, but I suspect that all churches are very diverse, though most of them do not admit it. I rather like the sentiment attributed to Queen Elizabeth I: "We do not want to make windows into men's souls." If we did, we might find out just how different from each other we all are.


## THE IMPORTANCE OF WATER

Churches can differ a lot, but they probably all want to refer to Jesus Christ in some way. To do this in the present day they will have to read the New Testament, which is the only record we have of Jesus, and they will probably want to have some ritual remembrance of the Last Supper, when Jesus, passing round bread and wine, said, "Do this in remembrance of me." It would also be silly not to know about the long history of Christianity, about the various interpretations of it there have been, and about what the major theologians and church councils have said. No-one can believe what every theologian has said, since they notoriously disagree among themselves. But at least you can get an idea of some different ways of trying to make sense of Christianity, and learn which ones seem to you to be not quite as silly as the others.

It is also generally agreed that when people join a church the sign of their acceptance is baptism. The Nicene Creed (I have not forgotten about it) says that "we acknowledge one baptism for the forgiveness of sins." There have been people who think this means that you have to be baptized if you are going to be "saved" (from hell, presumably). That seems to me to be rather silly. If God is even slightly loving, God will not say, "You will be tortured for ever unless you are immersed in water." Actually, in places where water is not available, you can have any suitably runny substance poured over you, and I know one or two courageous adventurers in foreign climes who have been baptized in tooth-paste, though probably not by total immersion.

Because baptism has been thought to be the means of forgiving your sins, and evading hell, there are people who have deferred baptism until they are nearly dead. They can then have their sins forgiven when there is less chance of their sinning any more (the Emperor Constantine is one of those people). There are also people who keep getting baptized so that they can be sure their sins can be forgiven over and over again. (I suspect that is cheating!)

There is no record that Jesus ever baptized anyone with water, but he is said to have baptized with the Spirit. That sounds more like it. If water baptism is a mediation of the Spirit to you, then that is not a matter of just getting wet. It is a matter of being placed in a new relationship with God, because God places the Spirit that was in Jesus within you. There is no point in deferring that, or in repeating it over and over. For it places you in a new relation to God, and the sooner that happens the better.

That is why many churches believe in the baptism of infants—not to save them from hell, but to make the point that God gives the Spirit of Christ to people even before they consciously recognize and accept the fact. Baptism is a sign of the unchanging and universal will of God to unite humans to the divine life by placing the divine Spirit within them. The gift of the Spirit is not confined to those who get baptized, just as the gift of eternal life with God is not confined to those who know about Jesus and go to church. But baptism is the gift of the divine Spirit to humanity. It is a historical sign of God's universal will to save, and it is a means of mediating that universal will in a particular historical situation.

You may wonder what the point of baptism is if everyone will receive God's grace anyway. That's a bit like saying: what's the point of getting married if you can have sex without being married anyway? The point is that you are making a lifelong commitment to another person "for better or worse" (though most people these days forget the last word). So, baptism is a lifelong commitment to God as God has been experienced in the person of Jesus.

There are all sorts of spiritual experiences in the world, some crazy, some sensible, some harmful, some helpful. Spirit can be experienced in many different ways, and those ways will partly depend on the personalities who have the experience and the societies in which they live. For Christians, Jesus is the person through whom a specific sort of experience of God was manifested and mediated.

There are lots of differing experiences of Jesus too. Some see him as a social revolutionary; some as a pacifist; some as an ascetic; and some as a "glutton and a wine-bibber"; some as a prophet of the end of the world;

some as a teacher of a mystical path of union with the divine. But there are limits, and it is hard to deny that Jesus was a critic of the religiously orthodox, that he ate with outcastes and sinners, that he forgave sins, taught obedience to God's laws and love of enemies, and proclaimed that the kingdom (the rule) of God had "come near." This gives a rather flexible range of possible experiences of Jesus with a central core of such ideals as love, humility, and forgiveness.

Churches are societies built around such experiences and core ideals. The Lord's Supper is a making-present of the risen and glorified Jesus— what I have called a manifestation and mediation of the same Spirit that filled the life of the historical Jesus. Baptism is the entrance into such a society, and it should be completed by a personal commitment to receiving that Spirit into your own life, and sharing in it with others. Christians can thus say that Jesus defines the Spirit of God; the communion meal mediates this same Spirit in a particular society; and baptism places you in that society where the Spirit of Jesus is mediated.

## BEGETTINGS AND PROCEEDINGS

The Holy Spirit is said by the Nicene Creed to "proceed from the Father and the Son." This might give rise to the idea that the Spirit is a different entity from God, who comes from God but is not quite God. Some early Christians did believe this, and there are still tedious and lengthy arguments about whether the Spirit proceeded *just* from the Father or from *both* the Father *and* the Son. The trouble is that "proceeds" is just a word invented for a process nobody understands, so what proceeds from what is bound to remain a mystery. How on earth can one argue about what one has agreed is a mystery? I have listened to long lectures on the subject, and still cannot tell any significant difference between proceeding from the Father alone and proceeding from the Father and the Son. I suspect that people were taking various verses of the Bible (usually from John's Gospel) literally. The verses were about God's relations to the creation, but people then tried to make them apply to God without any creation. The result is that you get all sorts of begettings and proceedings and relationships in a being that, according to the early theologians, was supposed to be changeless, not at all complex, and completely incomprehensible. There is apparently quite a lot going on in a being which is supposed to be changeless. No wonder many clergy are afraid to preach on Trinity Sunday!

It is much simpler to say that the Holy Spirit is in fact just God as present and known in and through human hearts and lives. Then we can say that the Father is God as creator of all things, the primordial source of all things; the Son is God as divine wisdom and love, expressed, manifest and mediated among humans in Jesus; and the Holy Spirit is God within us, uniting our finite lives to the divine. That is the Trinity in a nutshell. There is just one God, who exists and acts in these different aspects or ways of being.

Christians believe that God always exists in a threefold (Trinitarian) way, as source of all things, as supreme wisdom, and as dynamic life. And God is known to us in a threefold way, as transcendent "Father" or Creator, as divine Wisdom or Logos, embodied in Jesus, and as dynamic Spirit, who makes the spiritual reality of Christ present to us, relates us to God in a deeply personal way, and gives us a share in the divine life.

That may make it sound as though when you get baptized, you immediately start jumping around with excitement and speaking in tongues, as the disciples did at Pentecost. That does not usually happen, at least not in Anglican churches. In them, baptism is a much more sober and subdued event. Special people, called Sidesmen, are employed to make sure that people do not get too excited and enthusiastic, but sit quietly where they are put.

Nevertheless, something happens. Thinking of marriage again, the moment when you are declared to be married is not usually one of ecstasy—that comes later, one hopes. Something happens, and you are a new person with new commitments. In baptism, however quietly and unseen, you are also made a new person with new commitments. You are declared a child of God. God now relates to you as the Father of Jesus, as one with whom a fully personal relationship exists. You are made a "member of the body of Christ"—a way of saying that you are now a member of a society that is to manifest and mediate the love of Christ to the world. And you are promised that your life will be fulfilled in the "kingdom of God," the state beyond this life when you and those you love will know and love God fully and clearly.

It is true that God wants all people to know and love God, and all receive God's grace in one way or another. It is true that there are many religious and even non-religious paths that can lead in the end towards God. But a Christian church is a society with a particular calling and vocation in the world. It affirms that God is truly manifest in Jesus Christ, it aims to follow Christ's love and healing power in its way of being in the world, it claims to be inspired and empowered by God's love as experienced in a special way in and through the Spirit, and it proclaims hope in a world that can often seem hopeless.

A church is not a group of a few people who will go to heaven while everybody outside will be sent to hell, despite the fact that some bits of the New Testament, at their worst, show that some early Christians were tempted to take this very uncharitable view. If you look at the average church congregation, it looks a very odd choice of people to be selected for heaven, and not so very different from all the people who have gone to the beach instead, but are apparently destined in the long run to find things much hotter than they expected. No, the church is not a group chosen to be saved or to rule either on earth or in heaven. It is a group, a very mixed group indeed, who have been chosen to serve the world, to proclaim life, joy, and hope in an angry and often despairing world, and to co-operate with all those who work for good, whether they agree with them on obscure points of doctrine or not.

Baptism is a very good symbol for all this. As you descend into the water, you commit yourself to die to selfishness and greed, you are cleansed from all those things that separate you from a God of love, and as you come out again you are filled with the Spirit of the living Christ. That is the theory, anyway. It is such a good symbol that I think I am theoretically a Baptist, and I think you should be as fully immersed as possible, and be old enough to know the commitment you are getting into. I would be a Baptist, except that I do not like Baptist hymns very much, I have a taste for incense, and too many Baptist churches for my liking (especially in the USA) take the Bible too literally. That means I disagree with too many sermons for comfort, but I just have to sit there and take it. Members of the Anglican Church are much less likely to take the Bible literally, largely because they do not know what is in there in the first place.

In the Anglican Church infant baptism is still the norm. If you are going to baptize infants, I am in favor of the total immersion of babies for as long as possible—at least it keeps them quiet—but I have found that parents tend to be opposed to that. Some people think baptism is so necessary for salvation that there have been Roman Catholic societies devoted to baptizing abandoned babies, and of course Mormons baptize people who have been dead for a long time. I am not sure I see the point of that, unless you think that you have to be baptized to go to heaven. Some Roman Catholics have proposed a doctrine of "baptism of desire," in a rather expanded sense, which means that some unbaptised dead people would have been baptized if they had known what baptism really was. This, they say, can count as baptism. I suppose that is one way of explaining how God can want to save everybody, but can't do it because baptism is needed for salvation to work. It is rather like saying that everybody would have believed the truth if they had known what the truth was, but the fact is that they didn't know what the truth was, and when you are dead most people will think it is too late to find out.

I am rather uneasy about all this. It may be true that God's free grace comes before any human response, but to say that there need be no human response is taking grace a bit far. And babies make no response to being baptized, unless shrieking when the water hits the head is an acceptable response (and I have heard people say it is, because it shows the devil is being driven out). What is supposed to happen is that the baby will be brought up in a Christian home, so will naturally grow in a church environment, and the response will naturally grow as well. I understood how this view grew up, but nowadays it is a pretty unrealistic prospect. The Anglican Church tries to cope with this by offering a service of confirmation when people reach the age of reason. But when is that? A well-known Rabbi in England once said it is when the dog has died and the children have left home. Apparently, Catholics are twice as bright as Anglicans, because Catholics reach the age of reason at seven, whereas Anglicans do not and are not usually confirmed until they are about fourteen.

Anyway, I am reluctantly prepared to go along with this, because what it actually does is to spread out the baptism service over seven or fourteen years, and to tell the Holy Spirit to wait until a bishop comes along and finishes the lengthily postponed ceremony. In other words, the baptism of babies is not really a baptism at all. It is half of a baptism, which should end with the words, "To be continued later." It really makes more sense to start with a welcome of Christian children into the church, and later have adult baptism for those who are actually agreeing to accept the faith. But the churches have never regarded making sense as an important consideration in religion. And the way in which baptism has changed from being an explicit commitment of personal faith to being an initiating of young babies into a particular institution just shows how much things have changed since biblical times. In a strange way, this is actually helpful in showing that we cannot be content with just doing exactly what the Bible says. We have to be continually revising what we do and what we believe, and not be slaves to what people did and believed thousands of years ago. The old-time religion is just not good enough for me!

# CHAPTER SEVEN

## Death and Afterwards

### LIFE AFTER DEATH

ONCE YOU HAVE BEEN baptized and have joined a church where Jesus' death and resurrection is ritually celebrated, the theory is that you are, or you will be, "saved." That is, you will stop being filled with greed, hatred, and pride, and you will know and love God and everyone else and be wonderfully happy. As you look around your fellow members in church, you realize that this does not seem to be happening to any great extent. But then you might think, "Well, things could have been worse; and maybe they will get better." But if you look hard at your fellow members, and at yourself too, the chances of getting much better before you are dead look rather small. In fact, as you get older the chances of getting better seem to decrease. You begin to realize that if anything really good is going to happen, it will have to be after you are dead. For that reason—and also admittedly because Jesus was apparently seen after he was dead—most Christians come to believe that there will be some sort of life after death.

Persons exist and are special whether or not there is a life after bodily death. They might just have to die and stay dead for ever, whether they like it or not. But if there is a God who has planned a future of overwhelming good for the universe, there is some reason to think that persons, as finite co-workers with God, might actually get to see how that plan works out, and what it is like when it is complete. They might even get to be good and wise and really happy at last.

I have suggested that God (and, of course, lots of other people) might just have to put up with a great deal of suffering in any creatable universe.

We might feel slightly better about this if we think that God (who knows everything that can be known by a supermind) knows and feels the suffering that God's creatures feel. God is not just watching finite beings suffer in complete indifference. The suffering of creatures is not just possible. It is real. We might well think that it is only fair if God has to share in the suffering God has after all caused, even if God did not really want it to exist.

We all know about schoolmasters who say "This is going to hurt me more than it is going to hurt you" as they lay into you with a cane (well, at least people of my age know about this). Such schoolmasters, of course, are hypocrites, and they probably quite enjoy caning little children. We may hope that God is not like that. Maybe God cannot stop the suffering; but the least God can do is to share in it, since God caused it, after all.

That is one meaning of Jesus' crucifixion, to show that God shares in human suffering, and does not just watch it, whether with enjoyment or with no feelings at all (many ideas of God deny that God has feelings, but I reckon a supermind would have superfeelings).

Yet it is surely not enough just to have everybody suffering, including God. That seems worse than having nothing at all. In God's case, we know that suffering is not the whole story. We know that there has to be some suffering, but that God has a plan that will end in overwhelming goodness, though suffering just cannot be taken out of the plan.

God knows that suffering is necessary, given the creation God has chosen. God feels suffering in a vastly wider context of bliss and knowledge of goodness, which is part of the whole divine life. And God can foresee the certainty of an overwhelming goodness that is the goal of creation, and that could never have existed in the way it does without the long evolutionary process that has had to pass through suffering. In the long run, then, it seems to work out for God.

But what about us? Some human persons know little but suffering in their lives. They cannot see their suffering as an unavoidable part of an overall plan. They are not aware of the immense bliss of the divine being. And if they die they will never see the realization of the divine plan, or how their sufferings have contributed to it.

It would be a great good if each person could come to see how their lives fitted into the greater plan of creation, if they could see that plan realized, if they could share in that blissful end of all things. Persons could possibly do this, because they are capable of envisaging and understanding a cosmic plan, however vaguely. They can have a sense of purpose and of ideals that they ought to pursue. They can work with others in pursuing those ideals, and in making their own unique contribution to them. And if they ever get to see the plan realized, they can look back and see how all things, including their own lives, however imperfect they have been, have in the end been necessary to a full realization of the completed plan. Their earthly suffering will be placed in a wider context, which they will then see and understand, and it will be subsumed in a greater joy. That is something that seems to be possible, and if there is a God with enough power, there is good reason to hope it is true.

Such an afterlife would not just be for human beings. Any beings that are capable of these things would benefit from an afterlife. I do not suppose humans are the only such beings, but whether other animals on the earth are, I do not know. If we call the afterlife "heaven" or "paradise," then heaven will not just be filled with human saints, with a human Jesus sitting on a throne, and Mary his mother standing next to him as the Queen of Heaven. The Nicene Creed says that Jesus "ascended into heaven and is seated at the right hand of the Father." That sounds a rather boring job for Jesus, just sitting still for eternity.

It is, however, how it has been pictured in many traditional paintings. But heaven will surely be filled with personal creatures of millions of different sorts. The Eternal Christ, taking many finite forms, will be known to them all, and the transfigured human form of Jesus will be one of those forms. What that transformed human form will do I have no idea. But I would imagine that it would, like all resurrected lives, engage in endless creative activities and relationships. In that resurrection world there will be forms of life we can hardly imagine. There will probably be aliens from galaxies far away from ours. For all we know, there may be intelligent dinosaurs and highly advanced computers in heaven. I once became famous for five minutes by saying on the radio that I was prepared to baptize a computer. What I had in mind was not my own laptop, even though it can recite the Nicene Creed when I ask it. It was some future Artificial Intelligence that really did sincerely believe in God. Would it have to be saved by Jesus Christ? That depends on whether it had sinned or not, I suppose. If it was an impeccable computer, it would not need to have its sins forgiven, but it could still be "saved" in the sense that it could be liberated from its silicon casing and inserted into new and glorified hardware (spiritual hardware, of course). I do not believe in the resurrection of the iPad, but I could believe in the resurrection of a fully conscious and free Artificial Intelligence. I would certainly think that disconnecting it permanently would be murder. So, while I have my doubts about the existence of glorified and immortal potatoes, I have no difficulty in looking forward to getting to know a number of glorified and immortal computers. Indeed, it may be that they will be the only inhabitants of earth in a million years or so—though humans may still exist in zoos, to entertain baby computers on their days out.

## WHAT WILL WE BE LIKE AFTER WE DIE?

The last sections of the Nicene Creed talk about "the resurrection of the dead, and the life of the world to come." I am now going to go where the Creed fears to tread, and say what this is going to be like. If there is an afterlife, it will certainly not be like a Stanley Spencer painting, where some not very appealing and rather surprised physical bodies climb laboriously out of their tombs (dressed, it would seem, in their Sunday best). To tell the truth, I would not want to be stuck with my present body for eternity. Even if my arthritis could be eliminated, I would rather be young and virile again. Medieval thinkers agreed, and decided that everyone would be resurrected at the age of thirty-three. This is a pretty good age to be, usually. But babies who die very young may be considerably taken aback to find themselves instantaneously middle aged, and their parents would certainly have trouble recognizing them. "I didn't know you had a beard," they may cry, or more simply, "Who are you? I don't recognize you."

"I am your son. And I don't recognize you either, and I can't remember ever seeing you before."

"But you are the same age as I am."

"So is everybody else; we are all thirty-three. Where's grandma?"

"I am not sure. I never knew what she looked like at thirty three."

That is quite an unsatisfactory situation. Despite these problems, the medievals added that not only was everyone the same age, they were the *same size* too. Everyone would be a reasonable size, not too thin and not too fat but just right. One early theologian suggested that at the resurrection everybody would be perfectly spherical, since this, he thought, was the perfect shape. I once related this to an audience in the United States, and a voice from the back called out, "We're working on it, Reverend."

There is also, though I hesitate to mention it, the problem of flush lavatories. What are the toilet arrangements in heaven? Perhaps toilets will not be needed. Thomas Aquinas suggested that we will have stomachs and intestines, but we will not use them. We will also not eat animals, since if there are any animals there, they will be immortal, and therefore inedible. It looks as if lots of parts of our bodies will simply be obsolete. We would not need them.

I think we need to drop any thought of coming back to earth in a physical body. For a start, there would not be enough room on earth, unless there was a drastic cull of the population—which some Christians think there will be, since they think only good people get resurrected. Most Christians are more charitable and think that everyone will be resurrected —though I wonder how charitable that is, given that the same people often add that most of them will immediately go to hell.

It might be possible for souls to leave their bodies altogether, but then they would have little to do without bodies except things like looking up old memories of what they used to do when they had bodies to do things in, and doing mental arithmetic, which might become boring for most people after a few thousand years or so. Intelligent souls might well remember who they used to be, though most of them could still not solve differential equations.

There is no point in asking what disembodied cats and dogs would look like. You might think they would not look like anything, if they have no bodies. But there might be something like direct mental contact, which enables dogs to plant little pictures of themselves as they used to be into the disembodied minds of their owners. That is rather like people who play computer games, and plant "avatars" of themselves into other people's computer screens.

There is a problem of how the right pet dog would find the right owner if there were no bodily smells to help identify them. But there might be spiritual smells. I have no idea what spiritual smells would be like. Maybe they would be a bit like the smells or sights some of us have in dreams. Or they might be smells in a different form of spacetime (rather like a shared virtual reality world). That would be what Christians, Jews, and Muslims call "resurrection." If you have a good enough imagination, there is not a big problem about conscious creatures finding themselves in a different sort of space with different bodies, but remembering what they used to be like.

I don't see why all sorts of animals should not be resurrected and have quite a satisfactory life after death. And I don't see why resurrection should be confined to people who can do mathematics either. So why don't we just have resurrection for everyone and everything, even potatoes? Why do we have to say that only members of the human species have immortal souls?

I suppose you might say that there is not much point in being an immortal potato. Potatoes just wouldn't appreciate being immortal, or even know that they were the same potato from one moment to another. That suggests there is a reason for saying that only fairly complex sentient beings could appreciate having a life after bodily death. They would have to have a sense of continuing identity. That is, they would need to know that they were the same beings that they used to be. They would probably need to have a sense of continuing agency too.

I knew a PhD student who wrote a thesis entitled, "If I was resurrected, how would I know who I was?" A national newspaper included this in a list of the silliest doctoral theses of the year. But it is quite a serious question. After all, for all we know there might be many resurrected copies of my old earthly body. Which one would be me? I could hardly split up into lots of people, but there would not be any discernible difference between the copies. There might even be a body that had all my memories and personality, but would not be me.

I think the only answer to this is to say that if there is a God, God will make sure that there is just one resurrected body exactly like me. Moreover, my resurrected body will not be a copy of my earthly body. It will be a new spiritual body in a different spacetime, and I have not the faintest idea what it would look like. You might think that it would then be even harder to know if it was really me. I suppose I would remember doing all the things a certain body had done on earth, I would still have the same goals and ideals that body had (it is admittedly hard to see how I could pursue the same goals if I had a quite different sort of body, but presumably God can sort that out), and I would see how the actions that I had performed in that body had really been done by me, and had led to my having the sort of body I now had. In other words, I would have a sense of personal continuity. Unlike potatoes, I would know (or believe) that I have the same mind now that I had yesterday, and the day before, and even in a different spacetime universe.

All in all, I think it is possible for minds to transfer to different kinds of body. It would on the whole be a good thing if they did, because most of us think that we deserve something better than we have got now. Whether or not we deserve it, Christianity gives some hope that we will in the end get a much better body anyway.

## IS THERE A HELL AFTER ALL?

There is, however, the important fact that most of us actually did lots of really bad things, or failed to do many good things that we ought to have done. That is a bit more worrying. We spent a lot of our earthly time ignoring or even blocking God's plans for our world. No doubt we meant to love other people, but when we looked at them closely, we discovered that we really rather disliked them. What we cared about was mainly our own children, who used to be loveable little babies. Unfortunately, they too after a few years turned out to be pretty annoying adults, just like everybody else.

We also knew that we ought to share things out fairly. But we quickly found out that other people took more than their fair shares of everything, so we decided it would be stupid to let them walk all over us. The best way to do that was to get there before anybody else, take as much as we could, and if necessary trample all over the others in the process, in the nicest possible way, of course.

I remember driving up to a well-known restaurant one night, to find the car park already full of smart BMWs, waiting for the restaurant to open. When opening time came, all the drivers got out of their cars, and made for the entrance. Their dilemma was not to be so vulgar as to be seen to run to get there first, and yet somehow to manage to get there first as if by chance. It was an object lesson in British politeness, the object of which is to be seen to be quite unconcerned about one's own pre-eminence, and yet always to end up in front of everyone else.

It is much the same with revenge. Jesus said, "If someone hits you on the right cheek, turn the other cheek." But, as John Wayne would probably say, "If they hit you on the left cheek, then give them hell."

To cut a long story short, we have all pretty much messed up God's plans for how we should behave. And most of us feel that other people, if not us, should be punished in some way for the harm they have caused others. If heaven is a place of joy and delight, bad people should not be allowed in.

Imagine one Adolf Hitler arriving at the pearly gates. St. Peter says, "Welcome, Adolf. We are a very forgiving place, so we forgive you for all you have done. Come in and join the fun."

But Adolf says, "Are there any Jews here?'

"Yes, we have lots of Jews. There is an especially important one called Jesus. His mother is here too, and of course she is an important Jew as well."

"I can't believe it," says Adolf, "I thought they were Catholics." And he turns away in disgust.

The point of that story is to say that it is not God who excludes us from heaven. People exclude themselves, because they are not ready to enjoy being with the other people who are already there. If you do not like playing the harp, singing a lot, or having many improving conversations, you probably would hate heaven, so you have to go somewhere else.

Earlier in this book I got rid of hell, in the sense of a place where God tortures people for ever. But maybe there is a hell, if people whose lives have been filled with hatred and greed find themselves in a place where everybody is just like them, and where there is no restraining police force. "Hell is other people," said the writer Jean-Paul Sartre. It is certainly being with other people like us, when all social restraints have been taken away, and it is a matter of dog eat dog.

When you ask yourself what this sort of hell might be like, you have to think of what a cosmic mind that cared for the well-being of all creatures would do with creatures who messed up the carefully worked out plan for the cosmos. It is obvious that it would not torture them for ever. If we have to turn the other cheek, surely God cannot do less. On the other hand, they, being the sorts of people they are, cannot get into heaven.

Some sort of penal colony or training camp seems to be the answer. In the first section of chapter 1 of this book I mentioned three main images for such a place used by Jesus. One is a prison, where people stay "until they have paid the last penny." Another is a "fire," which burns away impurities. And the third is "outer darkness" (it is naturally grumpy Matthew who wrote this), where people exclude themselves from a great feast. They all imply that it might be possible to pay the last penny, or to escape from the fire, or to turn back to the light.

There has to be some form of deprivation of good. Hitler cannot just murder millions of Jews, and then relax in comfort for eternity. He has to see the enormity of his crimes, and he has to do something about them. He obviously cannot just put everything right; it is too late for that. But he has to do something that is hard, rigorous, and difficult, and that in some way improves the way the world is.

What is needed is a change of character and a rigorous training in good behavior. I reckon that with someone like Hitler that would probably take a long time, and success could not be guaranteed. If he kept on rebelling against the regime, he could call that hell, and it would no doubt be painful. The important thing is that he could always get out; it is up to him. Some people have called this "redemptive hell." It is a place of discipline and frustration of desire, but it is always possible to get out if you reform.

What seems likely is that in any case hell will not last for ever; the victory of goodness would never be complete while even one person continued to suffer, however much you may think they deserve it. That sort of punitive revenge is ruled out by the moral and loving character of God. The end of all things is the perfect and total triumph of love. That seems to require that if there are any who refuse to repent, they will in the end simply cease to exist, their personalities destroyed by their own hatred and bitterness.

I may seem to know quite a lot about the afterlife. The time has come to admit that these are all just educated guesses. I get the idea of resurrection, of judgment, and of a final goal of loving communion with God from the Bible, but I do not think there is just one consistent view of the afterlife in the Bible. What I am doing is saying what it would be good, as far as I can see, for a loving God to do if God creates a world containing creative and morally responsible persons. My imagination of what a loving God would do, indeed my belief that God is loving, has Christian roots. It is the New Testament that says, "God is love," and that spells out what love is in its records of Jesus. Jesus is said to be the judge of "the living and the dead." But he is also said to be the "saviour of the world." If our judge is also our saviour, that makes a huge difference.

Through all the unclarities, ambiguities, and even misunderstandings of the New Testament records throughout history, the teaching of the self-giving love of God stands as the central core of Christian belief. I believe that to be what is shown by the cross of Jesus Christ. But God has left us to work out what that implies for our lives on earth, and for whatever comes afterwards. Whatever we work out, we should never falter in our faith that the Christian gospel is one of hope, of joy, and of life more abundant. I still think fundamentalists get that right. The only trouble is they do not seem to see that this gospel is good news for everyone, not just for them.

# CHAPTER EIGHT

## Being in a Minority

### LIVING WITH DIFFERENCE

WHAT I HAVE DESCRIBED as the central core of Christian belief is really very simple. It takes no intellectual effort or love of argument to accept it fully and enthusiastically. So why have Christians spent so much time arguing with one another and condemning those who disagree with them about exactly which beliefs are acceptable? I suppose that once a set of people get together in a society, the first thing they are going to do is disagree with each other. That seems to be human nature. Maybe it is not all bad, because argument is a good way of refining our own views and getting clearer about the complexity of understanding the world and human life. It only gets bad when arguments lead to hatreds and the breakdown of human relationships. What is needed—especially in a society like the church, which is supposed to help us to love our enemies—is a way of learning to live with disagreements.

Especially in religion—where there is usually no way of deciding who is right and who is wrong, and where everyone admits that the whole thing is mysterious and on the boundaries of human understanding—any attempt to draw hard and sharp lines seems inappropriate. I imagine that anyone who wants to call themselves a Christian will see Jesus as the image of divine love and as one who gave his life in pursuing the goal of reconciling estranged human beings to God. They will want to practice a way of devotion to God as truly seen in Jesus. They will pray for the Spirit that was in Jesus to live in them, to make them better mediators of the divine love and wisdom. And they will hope for the eventual fulfilment of human life in conscious relation to God.

Do we need to get more technical than that? There is nothing wrong with trying to get a general view of the nature of things that will make the adoption of this way of life seem sensible, attractive, and conducive to human well-being. But what happened in the first few centuries of Christian thought was, first, that the New Testament documents were taken as literally as possible, and second, that the philosophical system used to interpret them was that of Plato and Aristotle, with its ideas of "substance," "person," and "nature," ideas that are highly controversial and nowhere to be found in the Bible.

For many of us, things have changed considerably. We cannot accept a literal interpretation of the New Testament—especially since the reported words of Jesus are so often metaphorical and picturesque, to say the least. And although we may admire Plato and Aristotle, their philosophy, at least in its technical details, has been rendered virtually obsolete by modern science. So many of us are not liable to be impressed by religious definitions that combine biblical literalism with archaic Greek philosophy.

In any case, that combination is impossible anyway. Aristotle thought God was changeless, timeless, and emotionless. The Bible suggests that God continually relates to people in personal ways, that God is often filled with anger, pity, and love, and that God grieves over the sins of the people. Christians even think that God "became human" and died on the cross, which poses severe problems for a changeless God who is unable to suffer or die.

Unfortunately, the early church produced a set of creeds that set out what all Christians were supposed to believe, and these creeds are often filled with archaic philosophy that most people do not even understand. The very short so-called "Apostles Creed" is just about comprehensible, if you interpret it rather freely. You might want to say, these days, that we do not necessarily have to refer to God as "father," since (as all early theologians agreed) God has no gender. God might not be "almighty" in the sense of "able to do anything," but is still as powerful as possible. Jesus may not have been literally born of a virgin. He did not literally rise up through the clouds to sit on a throne to the right of God, will not descend in the clouds any time soon, and on the last day our physical bodies will not come to life again and line up to be judged by Jesus. But you can get around all this by saying that these statements in the Creed can be taken metaphorically, not literally. Most people probably do this.

You can do the same with the Nicene Creed, and I have tried to do it in this book. Some might hesitate at the statement that Jesus is "of one substance with the Father," wondering exactly what a substance is, and what the difference is between "being begotten" and "being made." "Being begotten" seems to be a church invention that came about by an over-literal interpretation of the expression "Son of God." It is vastly misleading to many, since what is begotten is clearly different from what begets, and so seems to be a different substance. It also has no clear meaning in relation to a spiritual reality that has no gender and that certainly has no wife! The early church argued about this for years, before a rather unpleasant character called Athanasius won the arguments, but only after being deposed as a bishop and exiled three times. It was obviously a close-run thing, and most people have no idea of what the original arguments were all about.

The Athanasian Creed, which is also in the 1662 Anglican prayer book, but which I have never heard recited, borders on the absurd. Among other things, it says that in God there is "the Father incomprehensible, the Son incomprehensible, and the Holy Ghost incomprehensible . . . [but] there are not three incomprehensibles . . . [but] one incomprehensible." If that is not totally incomprehensible, I do not know what is. Yet the Creed ends by saying, "This is the Catholick Faith: which except a man believe faithfully, he cannot be saved."

It seems to be suggested that unless you can say, "This is totally incomprehensible; but I believe it firmly," you will not get to heaven. Fortunately, this creed has disappeared from more recent Anglican prayer books.

I am not suggesting that it does not matter what you believe. I am suggesting that this highly philosophical and detailed speculation about matters beyond human understanding is not necessary. What really matters is how we can get a right relationship with God, how we can live a life aimed at goodness and human fulfilment for all, and how we can have hope for the future in such a hopeless-seeming human world. Christians have been too concerned with "being saved," which is a form of long-term selfishness after all. They should be more concerned with how to save the world from destruction, how to obey God's law of love even for enemies, and how all people might achieve a union of love with God.

Speculate on the nature of God, the relation of Jesus to God, and the way to achieve union with God, by all means (in traditional terms, these are the questions of the Trinity, the incarnation, and the atonement, the "big three" Christian doctrines). If we are to have any hope of achieving reasonable beliefs, we need to support creative reformulations and non-threatening forms of argument, and make an honest confession of inadequate understanding. In other words, I do not think the "Catholick Faith" is what the Athanasian Creed says it is. I do not think the Christian faith is identical with the beliefs of any one institutional church or group of churches. I do not think it can be definitively captured in any one formula that excludes all other possible interpretations. If we have to have a creed, it should be much simpler and open to differing perspectives. Here is my own fivefold creed:

I believe:

in the creative consciousness of God,
in the revelation of the nature of God as love in Jesus,
in Jesus' death and resurrection as manifesting the divine
self-sacrifice and the reconciliation of humanity to God,
in the rule of the Spirit in human lives,
and in the hope of final human fulfilment in God.

That would do me—but this is not meant to be a formula that excludes everyone who is uneasy about it. It is meant to be one statement of what I think are the most important positive ideals of Christian life and thought. It invites further personal reflection and elaboration, but I would not expect it or anything like it to arrive at a full and finally adequate statement of the truth.

What church could I be in, given this viewpoint? The question is not really which church I could be in, but which church would put up with having me in it. So far the Anglican Church has managed that feat, probably by ignoring much of what I say. It is not by any means the only church I could be in, and it does not usually pretend to believe what the universal church has always and unchangeably thought (thank goodness, because there is no such thing). In many ways I love and admire the Roman Catholic Church, the biggest church around, with lots of wonderful people in it. I would be very happy to live as a Roman Catholic, but I think that church would be embarrassed to have me in it. It makes too many demands to believe things that I do not believe, like original sin and original guilt, the existence of eternal damnation, the authority of the pope to declare infallibly what is true, and the claim to exclusive possession of Christian truth. As a priest, I would have been excommunicated long ago. After writing this book, I may yet be excommunicated from the Church of England, but I suspect that Anglicans have forgotten how to excommunicate people.

Most churches, I have to say, are churches run by rather conservative old men (I am actually one of those), and I do not think such groups are best placed to convey Christian truth to the world. Perhaps the Anglican Church is not much better. But it does allow for a wide variety of diverse interpretations of the faith, from evangelical to catholic to liberal. It makes no claim to be the only true church. It is very supportive of critical and creative thought, while having a general respect for ancient traditions. It is very much a compromise church. But it has some extremely good music, some thinkers of intellectual stature, and some inclination to be a spiritual resource for people of very diverse outlooks but of moral commitment and good will. It also has lots of cucumber sandwiches and sausage rolls. That will have to do.


## CONCLUSION

In some important ways, the views presented in this book are pretty or-thodox. They suggest ways of thinking of God as Trinity, ways of thinking of a real incarnation of God in Jesus, and ways of seeing the death and resurrection of Jesus as authentic human expressions of the self-giving love of God that unites human beings to the divine life. However, these views are still likely to be rejected with horror by those who are committed to verbal formulations of doctrine that were issued long ago. I think that things have moved on quite a lot since then, and new ways of expressing Christian faith are needed. But churches are very reluctant to say that they have ever been wrong or inadequate, so they often like to stick to old phrases even when they no longer have a clear meaning. I have suggested using a different sys-tem, which I confess, rather late in the day, owes a lot to the relatively recent philosophy of Idealism. The German philosopher Hegel is the ringleader of this system. But Idealists do not have to slavishly follow what he says, which is just as well, since hardly anybody can understand exactly what he says anyway. More generally, Idealism is a system of philosophy that holds that mind is more real than matter, and that the whole material universe is an expression of a supreme eternal mind. Unfortunately, the heyday of this sort of Idealism was in the nineteenth century, and some people think it is now over. But people like me do exist, and I am pleased to say that the number of philosophical Idealists in Britain increased by 100% last year.

There are now about ten of us. This sort of Idealism sadly remains controversial both among philosophers and among theologians. The conclusion I derive from this is that we just all have to live with difference, defend the view that seems most adequate to us, but never pretend that ours is the only permissible opinion.

If you agree with this, the aim of having just one world church may not appeal. Those who want just one world church often seem to say, "We must all get together and love one another, and the best way of doing this is for you all to agree with me." It might be better to have a great number of churches, with different forms of worship, different statements of belief, and different understandings of faith. Jesus did pray that all may be one as he and the Father were one (John 17:11), but that is most unlikely to be recommending just one sociopolitical organization. (I do not think Jesus and the Father were anything like members of the same club.) It is more like appealing for a unity of mind and will about the really important things—the existence of a God of wisdom and love, devotion to Jesus as manifestation and mediator of that wisdom and love, dependence on the Spirit as the bringer of new spiritual life, and hope for the fulfilment of all creation in God. These are important things to agree on. There is plenty of room left after that for differences of temperament and social organization.

In short, I think the "one holy catholic and apostolic church" that the Nicene Creed talks about is not just one observable public institution. It is the spiritual ("holy") and worldwide ("catholic") set of societies that look to Jesus as the revealer of God and the mediator of ultimate human well-being (the basic "apostolic" faith). The ideal would be that the many diverse societies of this set, all of whose boundaries are fuzzy, would be united in a common trust, hope, and love that derives from the one they call Jesus the Christ.

The fact is that if you join any society you have to make compromises (unless you can start a new one, and even that will probably split before long). I am unlikely to agree with the whole of what any church says, unless I start it myself, and even then I would probably disagree with it quite often. As a matter of fact, I get on very well with literalists, as long as we do not talk about the creation of the world in six days, the second coming of Christ, the infallibility of the Bible, the existence of the devil, the acceptability of gay sex, and the fact that I am probably going to hell. I still love the literalists who brought me to Christ, so that list of disagreements, though it may seem rather long, does not touch our friendship, our common devotion to Christ and our life in the Spirit. We would not dream of burning each other at the stake (I think). We can be united in caring for the world that God creates and loves, and in seeking the welfare of all living beings, especially those less able to care for themselves, so far as that is possible. That is perhaps the best we can hope for. For me, at least, it is enough.

# APPENDIX

THE NICENE CREED, as it is written in the Church of England Prayer Book of 1662, which, being in Elizabethan English, is obviously the best translation ever, and what God really meant to say (but still not quite infallible).

I believe in one God the Father Almighty, Maker of heaven and earth, And of all things visible and invisible.

And in one Lord Jesus Christ, the only-begotten Son of God, Begotten of his Father before all worlds, God of God, Light of Light, Very God of very God, Being of one substance with the Father, By whom all things were made: Who for us men and for our salvation came down from heaven, And was incarnate by the Holy Ghost of the Virgin Mary. And was made man, And was crucified also for us under Pontius Pilate. He suffered and was buried, And the third day he rose again according to the Scriptures, And ascended into heaven, And sitteth on the right hand of the Father. And he shall come again with glory to judge both the quick and the dead: Whose kingdom shall have no end.

And I believe in the Holy Ghost, The Lord and giver of life, Who proceedeth from the Father and the Son, Who with the Father and the Son together is worshipped and glorified, Who spake by the Prophets. And I believe one Catholick and Apostolic Church. I acknowledge one Baptism for the remission of Sins. And I look for the Resurrection of the dead, And the life of the world to come. Amen.

\*\*\*

Written this day, very appropriately, on the Feast of Doubting Thomas, 2019.